MATH TRAILBLAZERS™

Grade
4

Unit Resource Guide
Unit 10
Using Decimals

SECOND EDITION

A Mathematical Journey Using Science and Language Arts

KENDALL/HUNT PUBLISHING COMPANY
4050 Westmark Drive   Dubuque, Iowa 52002

A TIMS® Curriculum
University of Illinois at Chicago

UIC The University of Illinois at Chicago

The original edition was based on work supported by the National Science Foundation under grant No. MDR 9050226 and the University of Illinois at Chicago. Any opinions, findings, and conclusions or recommendations expressed in this publication are those of the author(s) and do not necessarily reflect the views of the granting agencies.

Printed in the United States of America

2 3 4 5 6 7 8 9 10   07 06 05 04

LETTER HOME

Using Decimals

Date: _____

Dear Family Member:

In this unit the class will work with decimals so that students will have a better understanding of the meaning of decimals. We will use decimals by measuring length in meters, decimeters, centimeters, and millimeters. These measurement units are illustrated in the picture below. Linking our study of decimals with measurements will help your child visualize the relative size of decimal numbers. We will conduct an experiment, *Downhill Racer,* in which students roll toy cars or skates down ramps and measure how far the cars roll as we raise the ramp to

different heights. For this experiment, have your child bring a toy car, roller skate, or other "rolling toy" to school. Toys that roll straight and far work best. Please label your child's toy with his or her name so that there is no confusion when returning the toy.

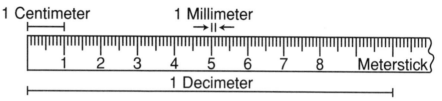

1 Meter is 10 Decimeters
1 Decimeter is 10 Centimeters

Meters, decimeters, centimeters, and millimeters

You can help your child by providing additional mathematics opportunities at home. For example:

- Help your child measure objects around the house in meters, decimeters, and centimeters.

- Talk about decimals in everyday life. Car odometers, labels on packages, and statistics in newspapers offer opportunities for discussing the meaning of decimals.

- Practice the division facts for the twos and threes with your child. Your child will bring home *Triangle Flash Cards* to study these facts.

Thank you for taking time to talk with your child about what he or she is doing in math. Please feel free to contact me with any questions, concerns, or comments about this unit.

Sincerely,

_____

UNIT OUTLINE

Estimated Class Sessions 12–14

Using Decimals

Pacing Suggestions

This unit will take 12 to 14 days to complete depending on your students' familiarity with decimals. Students began their formal study of decimals in Grade 3 Unit 15.

- Lesson 4 *Downhill Racer* provides connections to science. Students can collect the data for the lab during science time.

- Lesson 5 *Decimal Hex* is an optional lesson. It is a challenging game that provides practice comparing decimals.

- Lesson 6 *Alberto in TenthsLand* is an *Adventure Book* story that provides a connection to language arts. It is based on *The Adventures of Alice in Wonderland.* Alberto grows ten times larger than normal and shrinks to one-tenth his normal size. Students can read the story as part of language arts time.

Components Key: SG = Student Guide, DAB = Discovery Assignment Book, AB = Adventure Book, URG = Unit Resource Guide, and DPP = Daily Practice and Problems

	Sessions	Description	Supplies
LESSON 1 **m, dm, cm, mm** SG pages 270–275 DAB pages 163–166 URG pages 26–36 DPP A–D	2	**ACTIVITY:** Students measure objects in the classroom first to the nearest whole meter, and then to the nearest tenth, hundredth, and thousandth of a meter. They discuss appropriate units of measure for various situations.	• metersticks • base-ten pieces (skinnies and bits) • string • rulers • masking tape • envelopes
LESSON 2 **Tenths** SG pages 276–282 DAB pages 167–171 URG pages 37–48 DPP E–H	2–3	**ACTIVITY:** Students work with decimal notation for tenths. The emphasis is on connections between base-ten pieces, shorthand, and written notation for common and decimal fractions.	• base-ten pieces • metersticks • overhead base-ten pieces

	Sessions	Description	Supplies
LESSON 3 **Hundredths** SG pages 283–287 DAB pages 173–177 URG pages 49–61 DPP I–N	3	**ACTIVITY:** Students work with decimal notation for hundredths. The emphasis is on connections between base-ten pieces, shorthand, and written notation for common and decimal fractions. **ASSESSMENT PAGE:** *Linda's Base-Ten Pieces,* Unit Resource Guide, page 59.	• base-ten pieces
LESSON 4 **Downhill Racer** SG pages 288–295 URG pages 62–77 DPP O–V	4	**LAB:** Students collect, organize, graph, and analyze data as they study the relationship between the height of a ramp and the distance a car rolls. They measure the distance the car rolls using decimals. **ASSESSMENT PAGES:** *Roberto's Data,* Unit Resource Guide, pages 74–75.	• ramps • toy cars or skates • metersticks • blocks or books of equal size • masking tape • calculators
LESSON 5 **Decimal Hex** DAB pages 179–181 URG pages 78–80	1	**– OPTIONAL LESSON –** **OPTIONAL GAME:** As part of a game, students compare decimals.	• game markers • clear plastic spinners • base-ten pieces
LESSON 6 **Alberto in TenthsLand** AB pages 45–56 URG pages 81–88 DPP W–X	1	**ADVENTURE BOOK:** The hero of this story falls asleep in the library and has a dream about a place called TenthsLand. He has a series of adventures in which he meets several fantastic creatures. Decimals and 10 percent are emphasized.	• calculators

A current list of connections is available at www.mathtrailblazers.com.

Literature   **Suggested Title**

- Carroll, Lewis. *The Annotated Alice: The Definitive Edition. Alice's Adventures in Wonderland;* and *Through the Looking-Glass and What Alice Found There.* Introduction by Martin Gardner. Illustrated by John Tenniel. W.W. Norton, New York, 1999.

Software

- *Fraction Attraction* develops understanding of fractions using fraction bars, pie charts, hundreds blocks, and other materials.
- *Fraction Operation* develops conceptual understanding of fraction operations.
- *Graph Master* allows students to collect data and create their own graphs.
- *Ice Cream Truck* develops problem solving, money skills, and arithmetic operations.
- *Kid Pix* allows students to create their own illustrations.
- *Math Arena* is a collection of math activities that reinforces many math concepts.
- *Math Munchers Deluxe* provides practice in basic facts and finding equivalent fractions, decimals, and percents in an arcade-like game.
- *Math Mysteries Fractions* develops problem solving with fractions.
- *Math Mysteries Measurement* develops multistep problem solving with distance, weight, and capacity.
- *Math Workshop Deluxe* allows students to explore fractions and decimals.
- *Mighty Math Number Heroes* poses short-answer questions about fractions and number operations.

PREPARING FOR UPCOMING LESSONS

Ask students to bring in toy cars, roller skates, or other things with wheels for the experiment in Lesson 4.

BACKGROUND

Using Decimals

In this unit students continue to develop their conceptual understanding of decimals. They engage in a series of activities in which they learn to make connections between different models of decimals: physical models, pictures, real situations, symbols, words, and common fractions. See Figure 1. Translating among these modes of representation—drawing a picture to go with a display of manipulatives or reading "4.3" aloud as "four and three-tenths"—helps students develop a strong grasp of the meaning of a decimal, which enables them to maneuver between the many contexts in which decimals appear. Research indicates that students with a solid conceptual understanding learn procedures for working with decimals more easily and can apply those procedures to problem situations more effectively (Ball, 1993; Behr & Post, 1992; Hiebert, Wearne, & Taber, 1991; Lesh, Post, & Behr, 1987; National Research Council, 2001).

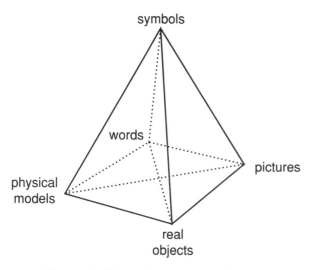

Figure 1: *Ways of representing decimals*

Models for Common and Decimal Fractions

This curriculum uses four main physical models for decimal and common fractions: the area model, the discrete model, the number line, and money. Each model illustrates decimals in a different way. Our goal is for students to become familiar with them all and be able to move freely among them. We discuss below the benefits and limitations of the different models.

The Area Model. In previous grades, your students worked with common and decimal fractions using area models, mostly rectangles, pattern block figures, and circles. We continue this work here, especially in the lessons *Tenths* and *Hundredths,* where students use base-ten pieces to model decimals. (Strictly speaking, base-ten pieces are a *volume* model for decimals, but pictures of base-ten pieces do approximate an area model.)

The area model is recommended for early work with fractions and decimals (Behr & Post, 1992). Children build on their everyday experiences (cutting toast, sharing pizza, etc.) when they use such models. Many real-life measurement situations (cooking, sewing, carpentry) involve fractions that are similar to fractions modeled with rectangles or circles.

The Discrete Model. In previous grades we also modeled common and decimal fractions with beans, cubes, or other counters. For example, if a dozen eggs is defined to be the unit, then one-half is six eggs, and so on. The number of eggs in one-half of 12 can be determined by separating the eggs into two equal groups and then counting the number of eggs in one group. Models such as this are called *discrete* because the quantities involved are countable. Quantities that are measurable—length, area, volume, mass, time, and so on—are not discrete; mathematicians call them continuous.

Base-ten blocks could be considered a discrete model, since we can find what is represented by each block by counting. Usually, however, when we think of discrete models, we think of distinct objects like beans or eggs.

The Number Line. Another important fraction model is the number line. Fractions on number lines, however, can be hard for some children to understand. For example, in trying to find $\frac{1}{2}$ inch on a ruler, a child might become confused by thinking about $\frac{1}{2}$ of the whole ruler. Another difficulty with the number line is that the end point of an interval is labeled, not the entire interval. So, for example, on a ruler $\frac{1}{2}$ would be marked at a distance of $\frac{1}{2}$ inch from the zero mark, but in a rectangle $\frac{1}{2}$ would be marked in the middle of the half-region. See Figure 2. These contrasting conventions can be confusing. To minimize these difficulties and to provide a real world context for decimals, our number line work is largely restricted to measurement situations like the *m, dm, cm, mm* lesson and the *Downhill Racer* lab.

Money. Another common and useful model for decimal fractions is money. Money is a useful model for decimals because children are so familiar with it. Children (and adults) have good intuition for situations involving money.

Certain conventions in our way of writing money, however, make its use problematic for beginning instruction in decimals. For example, we conventionally show exactly two decimal places when we write amounts of money (e.g., $4.50, not $4.5); normal decimal notation does not have such a constraint although this notation will be seen on calculator displays. One can also think of an amount like $4.56 in terms of two distinct units, dollars and cents. In this interpretation, the number before the decimal point tells how many dollars, and the number after the decimal point tells how many cents, thus making it harder for students to see the 50 cents as a decimal fraction of a dollar. This is analogous to the use of the colon in writing clock times: the colon divides two distinct units, hours and minutes. Other similar separators are used for feet and inches (4'6") and degrees, minutes, and seconds (47°15'45").

Operations with Decimals

At this point in their mathematical careers, students are developing their conceptual understanding of decimals. The work in this unit—skip counting, measuring, comparing to benchmarks, ordering, translating between various representations—is designed to build this basic understanding. Algorithms for paper-and-pencil addition and subtraction are not introduced until fifth grade, because a focus on standard algorithms at this stage would encourage students to attend to surface features of decimals and could hinder the development of deeper understanding. For most students in fourth grade, it will be more profitable to think through the few problems involving decimals that require computation rather than spending considerable time learning computational procedures.

When students encounter problems that require computations with decimals, urge them to invent their own methods to solve them or use a calculator. If students have a good understanding of the meaning of decimals and a good grasp of the problem situations, then inventing solution methods is feasible and instructive. This approach of developing conceptual understanding before focusing on procedures is consistent with the way we have developed the arithmetic procedures.

Figure 2: *One-half on a ruler vs. one-half of a rectangle*

Metric Units

The names of the metric units are logically constructed. There are three fundamental metric units: the meter (length), the gram (mass), and the second (time). (The liter and many other units are defined in terms of these three.) By combining these basic units with various prefixes, many convenient units of measure are obtained.

The prefixes come either from Latin or Greek. The Greek prefixes are used to indicate multiples of the basic unit; the Latin prefixes indicate subdivisions of the basic unit. So, for example, the Greek *kilo-* (1000) yields kilogram and kilometer, meaning 1000 grams and 1000 meters, respectively; the Latin *milli-* (1000) yields millimeter and milligram, meaning $\frac{1}{1000}$ meter and $\frac{1}{1000}$ gram.

Time is different from length and mass in that metric prefixes are only used for units smaller than one second. Metric units for times longer than a second (a 10-hour day, for example) have never been adopted.

Here are some of the most common metric prefixes and their meanings:

- micro- ($\frac{1}{1,000,000}$)
- milli- ($\frac{1}{1000}$)
- centi- ($\frac{1}{100}$)
- deci- ($\frac{1}{10}$)
- mega- (1,000,000)
- kilo- (1000)
- hecto- (100)
- deka- (10)

As students work with decimals, encourage them to share their strategies and experiences.

Resources

- Ball, D.L. "Halves, Pieces, and Twoths: Constructing Representational Contexts in Teaching Fractions." In T.P. Carpenter, E. Fennema, and T.A. Romberg (Eds.), *Rational Numbers: An Integration of Research.* Lawrence Erlbaum Associates, Hillsdale, NJ, 1993.

- Behr, M.J., and T.R. Post. "Teaching Rational Number and Decimal Concepts." In T. Post (Ed.), *Teaching Mathematics in Grades K–8: Research-Based Methods.* Allyn and Bacon, Boston, 1992.

- Hiebert, J. "Research Report: Decimal Fractions." *Arithmetic Teacher,* 34(7), pp. 22–23, 1987.

- Hiebert, J., and D. Wearne. "Procedures over Concepts: The Acquisition of Decimal Number Knowledge." In J. Hiebert (Ed.), *Conceptual and Procedural Knowledge: The Case of Mathematics.* Lawrence Erlbaum Associates, Hillsdale, NJ, 1986.

- Hiebert, J., D. Wearne, and S. Taber. "Fourth Graders' Gradual Construction of Decimal Fractions during Instruction Using Different Physical Representations." *Elementary School Journal,* 91(4), pp. 321–341, 1991.

- Lesh, R., T. Post, and M. Behr. "Representations and Translations among Representation in Mathematics Learning and Problem Solving." In C. Janvier (Ed.), *Problems of Representation in the Teaching and Learning of Mathematics* (Chapter 4). Lawrence Erlbaum Associates, Hillsdale, NJ, and London, 1987.

- National Research Council. "Developing Proficiency with Other Numbers." In *Adding It Up: Helping Children Learn Mathematics.* J. Kilpatrick, J. Swafford, and B. Findell (Eds.). National Academy Press, Washington, DC, 2001.

- Payne, J.N., A.E. Towsley, and D.M. Huinker. "Fractions and Decimals." In J.N. Payne (Ed.), *Mathematics for the Young Child.* National Council of Teachers of Mathematics, Reston, VA, 1990.

- Wearne, D., and J. Hiebert. "A Cognitive Approach to Meaningful Mathematics Instruction: Testing a Local Theory Using Decimal Numbers." *Journal for Research in Mathematics Education,* 19(5), pp. 371–384, 1988.

- Wearne, D., and J. Hiebert. "Cognitive Changes during Conceptually Based Instruction on Decimal Fractions." *Journal of Educational Psychology,* 81 (4), pp. 507–513, 1989.

Assessment Indicators

- Can students represent decimals using number lines (metersticks) and base-ten pieces?
- Can students read and write decimals to hundredths?
- Can students skip count by tenths and hundredths?
- Can students measure length to the nearest mm, cm, dm, and m?
- Can students collect, organize, graph, and analyze data?
- Do students demonstrate fluency with the division facts for the 2s and 3s?

OBSERVATIONAL ASSESSMENT RECORD

(**A1**) Can students represent decimals using number lines (metersticks) and base-ten pieces?

(**A2**) Can students read and write decimals to hundredths?

(**A3**) Can students skip count by tenths and hundredths?

(**A4**) Can students measure length to the nearest mm, cm, dm, and m?

(**A5**) Can students collect, organize, graph, and analyze data?

(**A6**) Do students demonstrate fluency with the division facts for the 2s and 3s?

(**A7**) _____

Name	A1	A2	A3	A4	A5	A6	A7	Comments
1.								
2.								
3.								
4.								
5.								
6.								
7.								
8.								
9.								
10.								
11.								
12.								
13.								

Name	A1	A2	A3	A4	A5	A6	A7	Comments
14.								
15.								
16.								
17.								
18.								
19.								
20.								
21.								
22.								
23.								
24.								
25.								
26.								
27.								
28.								
29.								
30.								
31.								
32.								

Daily Practice and Problems

Using Decimals

Two Daily Practice and Problems (DPP) items are included for each class session listed in the Unit Outline. The first item is always a Bit and the second is either a Task or a Challenge. Refer to the Daily Practice and Problems and Home Practice Guide in the *Teacher Implementation Guide* for further information. This guide includes information on how and when to use the DPP. A Scope and Sequence Chart for the DPP for the year can be found in the Scope and Sequence Chart & the NCTM *Principles and Standards* section of the *Teacher Implementation Guide*.

A DPP Menu for Unit 10

Eight icons are used to designate the subject matter of the Daily Practice and Problems (DPP) items. Each DPP item falls into one or more of the categories listed below. A brief menu of the DPP items in Unit 10 follows.

N Number Sense	**Computation**	**Time**	**Geometry**
D, I, O, P, R–V	H, K, M, N, X	N	F, J, L
Math Facts	**$ Money**	**Measurement**	**Data**
B–D, G, K, M, Q, W, X		A, E, F, I, L, T, V	

Practice and Assessment of the Division Facts

The DPP for this unit continues the systematic strategies-based approach to learning the division facts. This unit practices and assesses the twos and threes. The *Triangle Flash Cards* for these groups may be found in the *Discovery Assignment Book* and in the *Grade 4 Facts Resource Guide*. A discussion of the flash cards and how they might be used can be found in item B of the DPP. A quiz on the twos and threes is provided in item W.

For more information about the distribution and assessment of the math facts, see the TIMS Tutor: *Math Facts* in the *Teacher Implementation Guide*. Also refer to the Daily Practice and Problems Guides in the *Unit Resource Guides* for Units 3 and 9.

Students may solve the items individually, in groups, or as a class. The items may also be assigned for homework.

Student Questions	Teacher Notes
A **Measure with m or cm?** 1. List some things that you might measure in meters. 2. List some things that would be easier to measure in cm.	**TIMS Bit** Answers will vary and a wide range should be accepted.

Triangle Flash Cards: 2s and 3s

With a partner, use your *Triangle Flash Cards* to quiz each other on the division facts for the twos and threes. One partner covers the corner containing the number in a circle. This covered number will be the answer to a division fact, called the quotient. The number in the square is the divisor. Use the two uncovered numbers to solve a division fact.

Separate the used cards into three piles: those facts you know and can answer quickly, those that you can figure out with a strategy, and those that you need to learn. Make a list of those facts that are in the last two piles.

Put the cards back into one pile and go through them a second time with your partner. This time, your partner covers the number in the square. This number will now be the quotient. The number in the circle is now the divisor. Use the two uncovered numbers to solve a division fact.

Separate the cards again into three piles. Add the facts in the last two piles to your list. Take the list home to practice.

Circle the facts you know quickly on your *Division Facts I Know* chart.

TIMS Task

The *Triangle Flash Cards: 2s and 3s* are located in the *Discovery Assignment Book* after the Home Practice.

Blackline masters of the flash cards can be found in the *Unit Resource Guide* Generic Section. After students sort the cards, encourage them to practice the facts in the last two piles. As the class discusses strategies, emphasize those strategies that are more efficient than others. (See DPP items C and G.)

The Home Practice reminds students to bring home their *Triangle Flash Cards* for the 2s and 3s, and to study only small groups of facts (8–10 facts) at one time.

Inform students when the quiz on the 2s and 3s will be given. This quiz appears in item W.

Fact Families for × and ÷

The following four facts belong to the same fact family.

$3 \times 2 = 6$ $2 \times 3 = 6$

$6 \div 2 = 3$ $6 \div 3 = 2$

Solve each pair of related number sentences.

Then, give two other facts that are in the same fact family.

A. $3 \times 9 = ?$ and $27 \div 9 = ?$

B. $2 \times 10 = ?$ and $20 \div 10 = ?$

C. $2 \times 8 = ?$ and $16 \div 2 = ?$

D. $6 \times 2 = ?$ and $12 \div 6 = ?$

E. $10 \times 3 = ?$ and $30 \div 3 = ?$

F. $5 \times 2 = ?$ and $10 \div 5 = ?$

G. $1 \times 2 = ?$ and $2 \div 2 = ?$

Complete this item orally as a class. One student can solve the given facts and two other students can name each of the other two related facts.

A. 27; 3; $9 \times 3 = 27$;
    $27 \div 3 = 9$

B. 20; 2; $10 \times 2 = 20$;
    $20 \div 2 = 10$

C. 16; 8; $8 \times 2 = 16$;
    $16 \div 8 = 2$

D. 12; 2; $2 \times 6 = 12$;
    $12 \div 2 = 6$

E. 30; 10; $3 \times 10 = 30$;
    $30 \div 10 = 3$

F. 10; 2; $2 \times 5 = 10$;
    $10 \div 2 = 5$

G. 2; 1; $2 \times 1 = 2$;
    $2 \div 1 = 2$

D **Base-Ten Shorthand**

Write the following numbers or answers in base-ten shorthand. Use the Fewest Pieces Rule.

A bit is one whole.

A. 777   B. 4096

C. 2735   D. 20×2

E. 400×3 F. 30×3

G. 20×90 H. 600×3

A.

B.

C.

D. /|||

E.

F. /|||| /|||

G.

H. ◻◻◻◻◻◻◻◻◻

When Does $\frac{1}{4}$ Matter?

1. Might $\frac{1}{4}$ inch be important if you are building a door?

2. Do you think $\frac{1}{4}$ inch is important when you are measuring the distance you can ride on your bike?

3. Give an example when $\frac{1}{4}$ inch is important. Give an example when it's not.

1. Yes.

2. No.

3. Answers will vary.

 Counting Square Units

TIMS Task

1. How many square millimeters are there in one square centimeter? Use the picture below to help you answer the question.

1. 100 square millimeters

2. 10,000 square centimeters

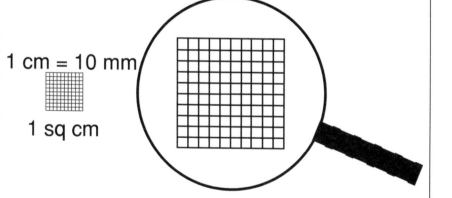

1 cm = 10 mm

1 sq cm

2. How many square centimeters are there in one square meter? It may help if you draw a picture.

Math Fact Practice

Solve the problem. Then write the other number sentences in the same fact family.

A. $15 \div 5 =$

B. $27 \div 3 =$

C. $16 \div 2 =$

D. $18 \div 2 =$

E. $21 \div 3 =$

F. $24 \div 3 =$

G. $2 \div 2 =$

TIMS Bit

A. 3
$15 \div 3 = 5$
$5 \times 3 = 15$
$3 \times 5 = 15$

B. 9
$27 \div 9 = 3$
$9 \times 3 = 27$
$3 \times 9 = 27$

C. 8
$16 \div 8 = 2$
$8 \times 2 = 16$
$2 \times 8 = 16$

D. 9
$18 \div 9 = 2$
$9 \times 2 = 18$
$2 \times 9 = 18$

E. 7
$21 \div 7 = 3$
$7 \times 3 = 21$
$3 \times 7 = 21$

F. 8
$24 \div 8 = 3$
$8 \times 3 = 24$
$3 \times 8 = 24$

G. 1
$2 \div 1 = 2$
$2 \times 1 = 2$
$1 \times 2 = 2$

Addition, Subtraction, and Multiplication Practice

Use paper and pencil or mental math to solve the following problems. Be sure to estimate to see if your answers make sense.

1. A. $148 + 779 =$ B. $2090 + 793 =$

   C. $7084 - 557 =$ D. $5386 - 737 =$

   E. $94 \times 7 =$ F. $38 \times 3 =$

   G. $57 \times 2 =$ H. $4068 - 843 =$

   I. $52 \times 9 =$ J. $87 \times 3 =$

2. Explain your strategy for J.

TIMS Task

1. A. 927
   B. 2883
   C. 6527
   D. 4649
   E. 658
   F. 114
   G. 114
   H. 3225
   I. 468
   J. 261

2. Possible strategy:
   $90 \times 3 = 270$ and
   $3 \times 3 = 9$;
   $270 - 9 = 261.$

 Number Line Decimals

The picture below shows a piece of a centimeter ruler enlarged. For each letter, write the decimal that matches.

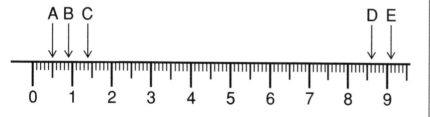

TIMS Bit

A. 0.5 cm
B. 0.9 cm
C. 1.4 cm
D. 8.6 cm
E. 9.1 cm

Line Symmetry

Parts of the pictures below are missing. The dashed lines are lines of symmetry. Copy or trace the pictures on paper and draw in the missing parts.

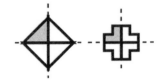

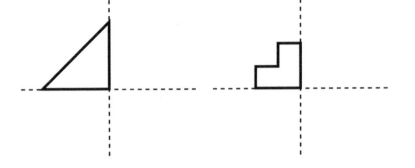

 The Price Is Right

Fill in the table. Find the largest second factor so that the product of the two numbers is close to the target number without going over the target number. The first has been filled in for you.

TIMS Bit

Students find the largest one-digit number that will provide a product that does not go over the target number. Students practice division facts by solving problems in which the division does not come out evenly.

Factor 1	Factor 2	Target Number	Left Over
5	7	38	3
3		28	
2		17	
7		25	
6		20	
9		48	
4		13	
5		12	

Factor 1	Factor 2	Target Number	Left Over
5	7	38	3
3	9	28	1
2	8	17	1
7	3	25	4
6	3	20	2
9	5	48	3
4	3	13	1
5	2	12	2

Student Questions	Teacher Notes

 Measuring Angles

You will need a ruler and a protractor to do these problems.

1. Draw a triangle. Make one angle 38°.

2. Draw a quadrilateral. Make one angle 125°.

3. Draw a hexagon. Make one angle 70°.

TIMS Task

Shapes will vary.

1.

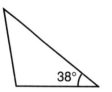

2.

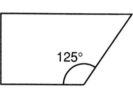

3.

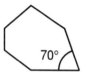

 Multiplying with Zeros

A. $80 \times 20 =$	B. $40 \times 3 =$
C. $3000 \times 40 =$	D. $20 \times 500 =$
E. $50 \times 30 =$	F. $600 \times 2 =$
G. $0 \times 20 =$	H. $10 \times 30 =$

TIMS Bit

A. 1600
B. 120
C. 120,000
D. 10,000
E. 1500
F. 1200
G. 0
H. 300

Time

1 day = 24 hours

1 hour = 60 minutes

1 minute = 60 seconds

1 week = 7 days

1. 5 hours = ? minutes

2. 4 weeks = ? days

3. 3 days = ? hours

4. $\frac{1}{2}$ hour = ? minutes

5. $\frac{1}{4}$ day = ? hours

6. $\frac{1}{10}$ minute = ? seconds

7. 360 minutes = ? hours

8. 42 days = ? weeks

TIMS Challenge

1. 300 minutes

2. 28 days

3. 72 hours

4. 30 minutes

5. 6 hours

6. 6 seconds

7. 6 hours

8. 6 weeks

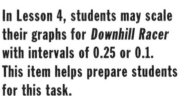 **Skip Counting**

1. Skip count by dimes to $2.00.
   Start like this: $0.10, $0.20, $0.30 . . .

2. Skip count by tenths to 2.
   Start like this: 0.1, 0.2, 0.3 . . .

3. Skip count by quarters to $5.00.
   Start like this: $0.25, $0.50, $0.75 . . .

4. Skip count by 0.25 (twenty-five hundredths) to 5. Start like this:
   0.25, 0.50, 0.75 . . .

TIMS Bit

In Lesson 4, students may scale their graphs for *Downhill Racer* with intervals of 0.25 or 0.1. This item helps prepare students for this task.

Be sure students say the numbers accurately. For Question 1, for example, they should begin, "10 cents, 20 cents . . . ." For Question 2, they should begin, "one-tenth, two-tenths . . . ."

Skip Counting by Tenths and Hundredths

1. Use a calculator to skip count by tenths. Skip count by tenths from 0 to 2.

   Press:

   Say the numbers quietly to yourself.

2. Skip count by hundredths from 0 to one-tenth.

   Press:

   Say the numbers quietly to yourself.

3. Skip count by tenths from 5 to 7.

   Press:

   Say the numbers quietly to yourself.

4. Skip count by hundredths from 2 to 2.1.

   Press:

   Say the numbers quietly to yourself.

TIMS Task

Be sure students read the numbers accurately. For example, in Question 1 students should begin, "one-tenth, two-tenths, three-tenths, etc."

The keystrokes listed work with most calculators that have the constant feature. Test your calculator to make sure that these keystrokes are appropriate for the model you use. If your calculator has the constant feature, each time the equal sign is pressed in the keystroke sequence for Question 1, for example, the constant number (0.1) and the constant operation (addition) are repeated.

More Fact Families for × and ÷

 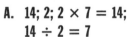

The following four facts are in the same fact family.

$4 \times 3 = 12$ $3 \times 4 = 12$

$12 \div 3 = 4$ $12 \div 4 = 3$

Solve each pair of related number sentences. Then, give two other facts that are in the same fact family.

A. $7 \times 2 = ?$ and $14 \div 7 = ?$

B. $2 \times 3 = ?$ and $6 \div 2 = ?$

C. $3 \times 8 = ?$ and $24 \div 3 = ?$

D. $6 \times 3 = ?$ and $18 \div 3 = ?$

E. $4 \times 2 = ?$ and $8 \div 4 = ?$

F. $3 \times 8 = ?$ and $24 \div 8 = ?$

G. $3 \times 1 = ?$ and $3 \div 1 = ?$

A. 14; 2; $2 \times 7 = 14$; $14 \div 2 = 7$

B. 6; 3; $3 \times 2 = 6$; $6 \div 3 = 2$

C. 24; 8; $8 \times 3 = 24$; $24 \div 8 = 3$

D. 18; 6; $3 \times 6 = 18$; $18 \div 6 = 3$

E. 8; 2; $2 \times 4 = 8$; $8 \div 2 = 4$

F. 24; 3; $8 \times 3 = 24$; $24 \div 3 = 8$

G. 3; 3; $1 \times 3 = 3$; $3 \div 3 = 1$

R Ordering Decimals

TIMS Task N

1. Draw each of the following numbers in base-ten shorthand. The flat is one whole. Then, put the numbers in order from smallest to largest:

    0.4   0.39   0.41   0.5   1.00

2. Draw each of the following numbers in base-ten shorthand. The flat is one whole. Then, put these numbers in order from smallest to largest:

    0.09   0.8   1.0   0.27   0.01

1. /|\ /|⠿ \|⠇ /\|/ ▢

    0.39, 0.4, 0.41, 0.5, 1.00

2. ⠿ /\|/\ ▢ |⠿ ·

    0.01, 0.09, 0.27, 0.8, 1.0

Student Questions	Teacher Notes

S Write a Decimal

1. Write a decimal:

   A. between 7 and 8

   B. between 1 and 2

   C. just a little bigger than 4

   D. just a little less than 2

   E. between $\frac{1}{2}$ and 0.8

   F. between 5 and 5.5

2. Explain your strategy for E.

TIMS Bit   **N**

Answers will vary.

T Which Length Is Longer?

1. Use a meterstick to help you answer the following.

   (Bits and skinnies might help, too. Remember, one bit is one centimeter long. One skinny is 10 cm or 1 decimeter long.) Which is longer:

   A. 2 cm or 11 mm?

   B. 32 mm or 3 cm?

   C. 5 dm or 45 cm?

   D. 2 m or 180 cm?

   E. 3 dm or 300 mm?

   F. 87 cm or 8 dm?

2. Choose one of the questions and explain your strategy for solving it.

TIMS Task   ⬛ **N**

1. A. 2 cm

    B. 32 mm

    C. 5 dm

    D. 2 m

    E. These two are equal.

    F. 87 cm

2. Answers will vary.

U Smallest, Largest, and In-Between

For the following base-ten shorthand, the flat is one whole.

1. ☐☐☐ ||||

2. ☐☐☐☐ |||

3. ☐ || ☐ || ☐ || ☐

4. ☐☐ /// ☐☐

    A. Which is the smallest?

    B. Which is the largest?

    C. Which are equal?

    D. Write numbers for each and put them in order from smallest to largest. (The flat is one whole.)

TIMS Bit   N

A. 1

B. 3

C. 2 and 4

D. 3.4, 4.3, 4.3, 4.6

V Metric Conversions

Change each of these lengths to meters. (*Hint:* Think of metersticks, skinnies, and bits.)

A. 327 cm   B. 405 cm

C. 5 cm   D. 87 cm

E. 10 dm   F. 24 dm

Change each of these lengths to centimeters.

G. 1.1 m   H. 1.01 m

I. 4 dm   J. 4.1 dm

K. 3.27 m   L. 0.4 dm

TIMS Task   N

A. 3.27 m	B. 4.05 m
C. 0.05 m	D. 0.87 m
E. 1 m	F. 2.4 m
G. 110 cm	H. 101 cm
I. 40 cm	J. 41 cm
K. 327 cm	L. 4 cm

Student Questions	Teacher Notes

 Quiz on 2s and 3s Division Facts

A. $8 \div 2 =$ B. $30 \div 3 =$

C. $16 \div 2 =$ D. $9 \div 3 =$

E. $12 \div 2 =$ F. $21 \div 3 =$

G. $15 \div 3 =$ H. $4 \div 2 =$

I. $10 \div 2 =$ J. $27 \div 3 =$

K. $14 \div 2 =$ L. $12 \div 3 =$

M. $6 \div 3 =$ N. $24 \div 3 =$

O. $2 \div 1 =$ P. $18 \div 3 =$

Q. $18 \div 2 =$ R. $3 \div 3 =$

S. $20 \div 2 =$

TIMS Bit

We recommend 2 minutes for this quiz. Allow students to change pens after the time is up and complete the remaining problems in a different color.

After students take the quiz, have them update their *Division Facts I Know* charts. Since students learned the division facts through work with fact families, it is likely that the student who answers $12 \div 2$ correctly also knows the answer to $12 \div 6$. To make sure, however, ask students to write a related division fact for each of the facts on the quiz (except $9 \div 3$ and $4 \div 2$). A student who answers a given fact correctly and who also writes the correct related fact can circle both facts on the chart.

A.	4	B.	10
C.	8	D.	3
E.	6	F.	7
G.	5	H.	2
I.	5	J.	9
K.	7	L.	4
M.	2	N.	8
O.	2	P.	6
Q.	9	R.	1
S.	10		

 Dividing It Up

$26 \div 8 = ?$ Write a story for $26 \div 8$. Then, draw a picture. Include any remainder in your picture.

TIMS Task

3 R2

A. Measure with m or cm? (URG p. 12)

1. List some things that you might measure in meters.

2. List some things that would be easier to measure in cm.

C. Fact Families for × and ÷ (URG p. 14)

The following four facts belong to the same fact family.

$3 \times 2 = 6$ $2 \times 3 = 6$

$6 \div 2 = 3$ $6 \div 3 = 2$

Solve each pair of related number sentences.

Then, give two other facts that are in the same fact family.

A. $3 \times 9 = ?$ and $27 \div 9 = ?$

B. $2 \times 10 = ?$ and $20 \div 10 = ?$

C. $2 \times 8 = ?$ and $16 \div 2 = ?$

D. $6 \times 2 = ?$ and $12 \div 6 = ?$

E. $10 \times 3 = ?$ and $30 \div 3 = ?$

F. $5 \times 2 = ?$ and $10 \div 5 = ?$

G. $1 \times 2 = ?$ and $2 \div 2 = ?$

DPP Tasks are on page 32. Suggestions for using the DPPs are on page 32.

LESSON GUIDE

m, dm, cm, mm

Estimated Class Sessions: 2

Students measure objects in the classroom to the nearest meter, decimeter, centimeter, and millimeter. Students also use decimal notation to record measurements through hundredths of a meter.

Key Content

- Measuring lengths in metric units (m, dm, cm, and mm).
- Representing decimals using base-ten pieces and number lines (metersticks).
- Reading and writing decimals to the hundredths.
- Understanding place value for decimals.
- Choosing the most appropriate unit of measure to solve problems.

Key Vocabulary

centimeter
decimal
decimeter
hundredth
meter
millimeter
nearest tenth

Materials List

Print Materials for Students

	Math Facts and Daily Practice and Problems	Activity	Homework
Student Guide		m, dm, cm, mm Pages 270–274	m, dm, cm, mm Homework Section Page 275
Discovery Assignment Book		*Class Measurement Tables* Page 163 and *Measure Hunt* Pages 165–166	Home Practice Parts 1 & 2 Page 155, *Triangle Flash Cards: 2s* Page 159, and *Triangle Flash Cards: 3s* Page 161
Facts Resource Guide	DPP Items 10B, 10C & 10D Use the *Triangle Flash Cards: 2s* and *Triangle Flash Cards: 3s* to review the division facts for these groups.		
Unit Resource Guide	DPP Items A–D Pages 12–14		

Student Books spans the Student Guide and Discovery Assignment Book rows.
Teacher Resources spans the Facts Resource Guide and Unit Resource Guide rows.

available on Teacher Resource CD

All Transparency Masters, Blackline Masters, and Assessment Blackline Masters in the Unit Resource Guide are on the Teacher Resource CD.

Supplies for Each Student

centimeter ruler
string, enough for 1 m for each student
envelope for storing flash cards

Supplies for Each Student Group

1 or 2 metersticks
skinnies and bits, about 10 of each

Materials for the Teacher

Transparency of *Class Measurement Tables* Activity Page (Discovery Assignment Book) Page 163
Observational Assessment Record (Unit Resource Guide, Pages 9–10 and Teacher Resource CD)
masking tape

m, dm, cm, mm

Meters (m)

Your teacher has made marks 1 and 2 **meters** above the floor. Use these marks to help you answer the questions below.

1. Are you more than 1 meter tall?

2. Are you more than 2 meters tall?

3. Are you closer to 1 meter or 2 meters?

4. As a class, measure objects around the classroom to the nearest whole meter. The symbol for meter is **m**. Keep track of the data on the *Class Measurement Tables* in the *Discovery Assignment Book*.

Class Measurement Table

Object	Measurement (nearest m)
Height of door	
Width of classroom	
Length of classroom	
Width of chalkboard	
Length of paper clip	
Length of pencil	

Student Guide - Page 270

Measurements to the Nearest Meter Data Table

Object	Measurement (nearest m)
Height of door	2
Width of classroom	8
Length of classroom	14
Width of chalkboard	5
Length of paper clip	0
Length of pencil	0

Figure 3: *Measurements to the nearest meter data table*

Before the Activity

Place a piece of tape on a wall or a door 1 meter from the floor and another piece 2 meters from the floor in a location that is visible to all students. (These will be used for estimating heights using the benchmarks 1 m and 2 m.) Cut pieces of string one meter long, one for each student or have students measure and cut strings at the end of Part 1.

Developing the Activity

This activity leads students through measuring the same objects several times with progressively smaller units. Students are led to see that it is usually unsatisfactory to measure small objects such as paper clips or pencils to the nearest whole meter. When we use too gross a measure, we get very little useful information. If I tell you how many miles long my living room is to the nearest whole mile, you don't know much. If I tell you how many light-years it is to the nearest whole light-year from Chicago to Paducah, that doesn't help much either. Choosing the appropriate unit of measure, e.g., miles for Chicago to Paducah, feet for a living room, etc., helps make sense of the measurement.

Part 1. Meters and Decimeters

The Meters section of the *m, dm, cm, mm* Activity Pages in the *Student Guide* introduces the notion of measuring to the nearest meter. In *Question 4,* the class completes a data table in the *Discovery Assignment Book* with measurements of objects in the classroom as shown in Figure 3. Record students' measurements on a transparency of the *Class Measurement Tables* Activity Page.

In the later parts of this activity, these same objects are measured using smaller units. Different class data tables should be created each time instead of adding columns to the first table. If the measurement for height of a door is recorded as 2 meters and then recorded as 19 decimeters in the same table, students may mistakenly think the height is 2 meters 19 decimeters.

TIMS Tip

To avoid having students group around certain objects or having students wandering looking for objects to measure, make a list of classroom objects that students can measure. Assign groups of students to measure certain objects.

Question 8 asks how many skinnies can you line up along a meterstick. Ask:

- *If a decimeter is one-tenth, then what is one whole?* Ten decimeters make a meter.
- *If a skinny is one-tenth of a whole unit, what base-ten piece represents the whole?* Ten skinnies make a flat.

Question 11 asks students to remeasure the objects they have measured to the nearest meter, but this time they measure to the nearest decimeter using metersticks and skinnies. This data should be recorded in the appropriate data table on the *Class Measurement Tables* Activity Page. Discuss the differences between the two tables.

Another way to foster intuitions about length is to identify reference lengths for different units of measure. For example, when students think of a meter, they could think of the distance between the floor and a doorknob. Ask:

- *What object do you think of when I say, How long is a centimeter?*
- *A millimeter?*
- *A decimeter?*
- *A meter?*

Ideas for "unit reference lengths" can be listed on a bulletin board.

At this point in the lesson, you can assign *Questions 1–2* in the Homework section of the *m, dm, cm, mm* Activity Pages in the *Student Guide.* They are designed to help students develop intuitions about the metric system and the length of a meter. Students can use their meter-length strings or regular metersticks to measure.

Content Note

The **decimeter** is a metric unit that is not commonly used in the United States. We include it here for completeness and because sometimes it is the best unit to use. The centimeter is more commonly used for small lengths; however, even whole centimeters are too large for tiny lengths like the thickness of a penny, the thickness of a piece of hair, or the thickness of a compact disc. For these we use millimeters or even smaller units.

Class Measurement Tables

Name _____ Date _____

To the Nearest Meter

Object	Measurement (nearest m)
Height of Door	
Width of Classroom	
Length of Classroom	
Width of Chalkboard	
Length of Paper Clip	
Length of Pencil	

To the Nearest Decimeter

Object	Measurement (nearest dm)
Height of Door	
Width of Classroom	
Length of Classroom	
Width of Chalkboard	
Length of Paper Clip	
Length of Pencil	

To the Nearest Centimeter

Object	Measurement (nearest cm)
Height of Door	
Width of Classroom	
Length of Classroom	
Width of Chalkboard	
Length of Paper Clip	
Length of Pencil	

m, dm, cm, mm   DAB · Grade 4 · Unit 10 · Lesson 1 163

Copyright © Kendall/Hunt Publishing Company

Discovery Assignment Book - Page 163

---

5. Jackie measured her calculator to the nearest meter and found it to be 0 meters long. What does this measurement (0 m) tell you? What unit would give you a better measurement for this length?

6. Sometimes it is good enough to measure to the nearest whole meter. Sometimes it is not. Usually, it does not make sense to measure a calculator to the nearest meter. List two things that probably should not be measured to the nearest meter.

7. List two things that you would measure to the nearest meter.

Decimeters (dm)

8. How many skinnies can you line up on a meterstick? Line them up along a meterstick to find out.

9. The length of one skinny is a **decimeter**. The symbol for decimeter is **dm**. How many dm are in 1 meter? How many dm are in $\frac{1}{2}$ meter?

10. A decimeter is $\frac{1}{10}$ of a meter. What do you think **deci-** means?

11. As a class, measure the objects in the table from Question 4 again, but this time to the nearest whole decimeter. Make a new table for this data like the one shown below.

Class Measurement Table

Object	Measurement (nearest dm)
Height of door	
Width of classroom	
Length of classroom	

m, dm, cm, mm   SG · Grade 4 · Unit 10 · Lesson 1 271

Student Guide - Page 271

12. John measured a paper clip to the nearest decimeter and found it to be 0 decimeters long. What information does this measurement tell you? What unit would give you a better measurement for a paper clip?

13. Sometimes it is good enough to measure to the nearest whole decimeter. Sometimes it is not. List two things that should be measured to the nearest decimeter.

Centimeters (cm)

A **cent**ury is 100 years; a **cent**ennial is a 100-year anniversary; a **cent**ipede is said to have 100 legs. What do you think **cent-** means?

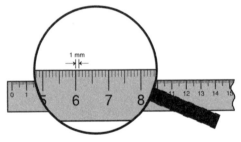

A **cent**imeter is $\frac{1}{100}$ of a meter and a **cent** is $\frac{1}{100}$ of a dollar. In other words, there are 100 centimeters in a meter and 100 cents in a dollar.

14. How many bits can you line up along a meterstick? How did you decide?

15. How long is a bit?

16. As a class, measure the objects from Question 4 again, but this time measure to the nearest whole centimeter. Make a new table for this data like the one shown below.

17. List two things it makes sense to measure to the nearest whole centimeter. List two things it does not make sense to measure in centimeters.

Class Measurement Table

Object	Measurement (nearest cm)
Height of door	
Width of classroom	
Length of classroom	

18. Find an object that measures less than 1 centimeter.

Student Guide - Page 272

Millimeters (mm)

If you look at a meterstick very carefully, you will see little spaces between short lines. Each one of these spaces is a millimeter.

19. There are 1000 **milli**meters in a meter. What do you think **milli-** means?

20. How many millimeters are in a centimeter?

21. How many millimeters are in a decimeter? How did you decide?

22. People generally use millimeters to measure very short lengths. Give an example of when it would make sense to measure in millimeters.

Measuring with Metersticks, Skinnies, and Bits

John measured the length of the chalkboard in his classroom. First, he used two metersticks. He saw that less than half of a third meterstick would fit. John said, "To the nearest whole meter, this length is 2 meters."

Student Guide - Page 273

Part 2. Centimeters and Millimeters

Students measure the objects again, this time to the nearest centimeter using metersticks and bits. The results should be displayed in a third class data table. A comparison of the three tables should be instructive.

Use the Centimeters section of the *m, dm, cm, mm* Activity Pages to direct your discussion.

After completing **Question 16,** you might ask students why they think they are not asked in the Centimeters part of the *m, dm, cm, mm* Activity Pages to measure the objects in their data tables to the nearest millimeter. They should see that in most cases it may be difficult and not necessary to measure larger objects to the nearest millimeter. See the TIMS Tutor: *Estimation, Accuracy, and Error* in the *Teacher Implementation Guide* for more information.

After students answer **Question 22,** ask:

- *How would you record 1 decimeter as part of a meter?* (0.1 m)
- *How would you record 1 centimeter as part of a meter?* (0.01 m)
- *How would you record 1 millimeter as part of a meter?* (0.001 m)

Both decimal and common fractions should be discussed. The *m, dm, cm, mm* Activity Pages reinforce and build upon this discussion.

Content Note

Reading Decimals. The symbols *4.3* are usually read as "four and three-tenths" or "four point three." Either reading is correct, but we prefer the former at this stage because it makes the connection with fractions explicit. We want students to think of decimals as fractions, not merely as strings of symbols.

Journal Prompt

Most door handles are about one meter from the floor. Why do you think this is? Can you think of another example of something that is almost always made the same size?

Part 3. *Measure Hunt*

Use the Measuring with Metersticks, Skinnies, and Bits section in the *Student Guide* to introduce a slight variation of the Fewest Pieces Rule using bits, skinnies, and metersticks. In measuring, students should use as many metersticks as possible, then as many skinnies as possible, and then as many bits as possible. This will result in measuring with the fewest number of pieces.

After completing **Question 23** in the *Student Guide*, students complete the *Measure Hunt* Activity Pages in the *Discovery Assignment Book*. Students will measure objects in the room to the nearest hundredth of a meter. Each group of students will need 2 metersticks, 8–10 skinnies, 10 bits, and the *Measure Hunt* Activity Pages. First, students measure using metersticks, skinnies, and bits and record the data on Table 1. Then, students measure other objects using only metersticks and record the data on Table 2.

Next John put down four skinnies. John said, "Each meterstick is ten decimeters, and each skinny is one decimeter long. I have two metersticks and four skinnies. So, to the nearest decimeter, this length is 24 whole decimeters."

John still had a little space left. He put down one bit. One bit is one centimeter long.

Mrs. Dewey complimented John's work: "John, you have done a terrific job. You have found the length of the chalkboard using the fewest pieces. You can write down this measurement using decimals. How many metersticks did you use?" "Two," said John.

Mrs. Dewey wrote "2." on the board. "Each decimeter is one-tenth of a meter. How many skinnies did you use?" "Four," said John.

Mrs. Dewey wrote "2.4" on the board. "Each centimeter is one-hundredth of a meter. How many bits did you use?" "One," said John.

Mrs. Dewey wrote "2.41" on the board. "This number is read two and forty-one hundredths." John showed 2.41 m with two metersticks, four skinnies, and 1 bit.

John continued to measure objects around the room to the nearest hundredth of a meter. For example, Mrs. Dewey had a life-size poster of a professional basketball player on the wall. John decided to measure the height of this player. He used 1 meterstick, 9 skinnies, and 8 bits. John wrote "1.98 meters" for this measurement. That told him the player's height was 1 meter, 9 decimeters, and 8 centimeters.

23. John wrote the following measurements on his paper. He used the fewest pieces for each measurement. How many metersticks, skinnies, and bits did John use for each measurement?

   A. 3.45 m
   B. 0.59 m
   C. 2.70 m
   D. 2.07 m

Student Guide - Page 274

Name _____   Date _____

Measure Hunt

Find four lengths in the classroom using the rules in the table below. Use the fewest pieces possible when you measure. Use metersticks to measure meters. Use skinnies to measure decimeters. Use bits to measure centimeters. Then, complete the table. An example is done for you.

Table 1

Rule	Object	Number of			Length (nearest 0.01 m)
		m	dm	cm	
Between 1 and 2 m	Height of cabinet	1	2	0	1.20
Between 1 and 1.5 m					
Between 0.5 and 1 m					
Between 0.5 and 0.8 m					
Between 0.55 and 0.75 m					

Discovery Assignment Book - Page 165

Name _____   Date _____

Find five lengths in the classroom using the rules in the table below. Use metersticks to measure the lengths. Then, complete the table.

Table 2

Rule	Object	Number of			Length (nearest 0.01 m)
		m	dm	cm	
Between 1 and 2 m					
Between 1 and 1.5 m					
Between 0.5 and 1 m					
Between 0.6 and 0.9 m					
Between 0.40 and 0.65 m					

Discovery Assignment Book - Page 166

Daily Practice and Problems:
Tasks for Lesson 1

B. Task: *Triangle Flash Cards: 2s and 3s*
(URG p. 13)

With a partner, use your *Triangle Flash Cards* to quiz each other on the division facts for the twos and threes. One partner covers the corner containing the number in a circle. This covered number will be the answer to a division fact, called the quotient. The number in the square is the divisor. Use the two uncovered numbers to solve a division fact.

Separate the used cards into three piles: those facts you know and can answer quickly, those that you can figure out with a strategy, and those that you need to learn. Make a list of those facts that are in the last two piles.

Put the cards back into one pile and go through them a second time with your partner. This time, your partner covers the number in the square. This number will now be the quotient. The number in the circle is now the divisor. Use the two uncovered numbers to solve a division fact.

Separate the cards again into three piles. Add the facts in the last two piles to your list. Take the list home to practice.

Circle the facts you know quickly on your *Division Facts I Know* chart.

D. Task: Base-Ten Shorthand
(URG p. 14)

Write the following numbers or answers in base-ten shorthand. Use the Fewest Pieces Rule.

A bit is one whole.

A. 777	B. 4096
C. 2735	D. 20×2
E. 400×3	F. 30×3
G. 20×90	H. 600×3

Suggestions for Teaching the Lesson

Math Facts

- DPP Task B reminds students to practice the division facts for the twos and threes. Bit C provides practice with fact families. Task D provides practice writing numbers in base-ten shorthand as well as practice multiplying with multiples of 10.

- Part 1 of the Home Practice reminds students to practice division facts for the twos and threes using their *Triangle Flash Cards*.

Homework and Practice

- Assign *Questions 1–2* in the Homework section on the *m, dm, cm, mm* Activity Pages after Part 1. Assign *Question 3* after Part 3. Students will need their meter strings to help in their measurements.

- DPP Bit A asks students to consider how to choose appropriate units of measure.

- Assign Part 2 of the Home Practice. It includes computation, rounding, and estimation practice.

Answers for Part 2 of the Home Practice can be found in the Answer Key at the end of this lesson and at the end of this unit.

Homework

Dear Family Member:

In everyday life in the United States, we are slowly moving toward regular use of metric measurements. In scientific life, however, the metric system is already here. To succeed in a technological world, students need to know the metric system. This homework assignment will help your child become aware of the increasing use of metric units.

Thank you for your cooperation.

Even though we often use customary units of measure (inches, pints, pounds, and so on) in everyday life, there are many times we use metric units of measure (centimeters, liters, grams, and so on).

1. Look for metric units in the newspaper, on labels, and around the house. Make a list showing what the unit is and what is being measured. If you can, bring in the paper with the measurement on it.

2. A. Cut a piece of string 1 meter long.
   B. Carry your meter string with you all the time for one week.
   C. Estimate the length of various objects to the nearest meter. Then, use your meter string to measure the objects to the nearest meter. Make a table showing the objects, your estimates, and your measurements.

3. Go on a measure hunt in your home. Look for objects that are between the specified lengths. Complete a data table like this one. (*Hint*: Half of your string is 0.5 m.)

Rule	Object
Between 1 and 2 m	
Between 1 and 1.5 m	
Between 0.5 and 1 m	

m, dm, cm, mm   SG · Grade 4 · Unit 10 · Lesson 1 275

Student Guide - Page 275

Assessment

- Observe whether students can measure to the nearest mm, cm, dm, and m. Record your observations on the *Observational Assessment Record*.

- Another way to find out whether students can measure accurately is by setting up a performance assessment. First, identify standard objects that all students can measure simultaneously. For example, ask students to measure any of the following:

  1. the length and width of their desks
  2. the length and width of their *Student Guides*
  3. the length of a standard paper clip
  4. the length and width of a piece of paper
  5. the length of a chalkboard or a bulletin board

     Let students find the appropriate unit of length for each object and then have them carry out the measurements.

Extension

- Students should estimate lengths throughout the course of this unit. One type of estimate is a judgment whether an object is longer or shorter than some benchmark: Is your desk wider than 30 cm? How do you know? Is your arm longer or shorter than one meter? How do you know? Another type of estimate is a rough judgment of a length: Estimate the length of your foot in decimeters. Now estimate your foot in centimeters. Would it make sense to estimate the length of your foot in millimeters? Checking estimates by measuring will improve both estimation and measurement skills.

- Ask students to draw a line that is two decimeters long. Then ask them to attach a 3 cm line and a 5 millimeter line to it. What is the total length of the line in millimeters? Centimeters? Decimeters? Repeat for other lengths.

- What is 17 mm plus 4 cm? (It is not 21 anything.) Draw a 17 mm line and then attach a 4 cm line to it. Students can write their answer in mm and in cm. Repeat for other lengths.

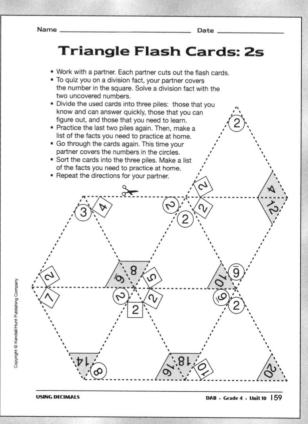

Discovery Assignment Book - Page 155

Discovery Assignment Book - Page 159

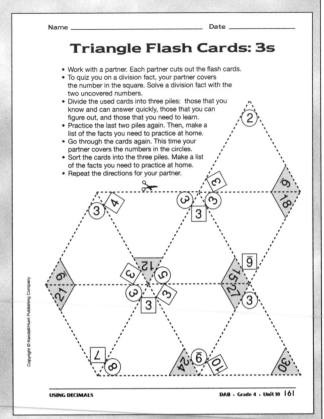

Discovery Assignment Book - Page 161

AT A GLANCE

Math Facts and Daily Practice and Problems

DPP items B and C provide practice with division facts. Task D provides practice with base-ten shorthand and multiplying with multiples of 10. Bit A requires consideration of appropriate units of measure.

Part 1. Meters and Decimeters

1. Place a piece of tape on a door or wall 1 meter (m) above the floor and a second piece 2 meters above the floor.

2. Students determine if their heights are closer to 1 m or 2 m. (*Questions 1–3* in the *Student Guide*)

3. Students measure objects to the nearest m. (*Question 4*)

4. Students record their measurements on the *Class Measurement Tables* Activity Page in the *Discovery Assignment Book*.

5. Discuss when it is appropriate to measure to the nearest meter. (*Questions 5–6*)

6. Students line 10 skinnies along a meterstick. (*Question 8*)

7. Discuss the prefix *deci-* and the word decimeter (dm). (*Questions 9–10*)

8. Students measure objects to the nearest dm. A class data table is created. (*Question 11*)

9. Discuss when it is appropriate to measure to the nearest decimeter. (*Questions 12–13*)

AT A GLANCE

Part 2. Centimeters and Millimeters

1. Discuss the prefix *centi-* and the word centimeter (cm).
2. Students determine that they can line up 100 bits along a meter. *(Questions 14–15)*
3. Students measure objects to the nearest cm. A class table is created. *(Question 16)*
4. Discuss when it is appropriate to measure to the nearest centimeter. *(Questions 17–18)*
5. Discuss the prefix *milli-* and the use of millimeters (mm). *(Questions 19–22)*

Part 3. *Measure Hunt*

1. Students read and discuss the Measuring with Metersticks, Skinnies, and Bits section in the *Student Guide.* Discuss John's measurements, the Fewest Pieces Rule, and how to use decimals to record measurements. Complete *Question 23.*
2. Students use the *Measure Hunt* Activity Pages in the *Discovery Assignment Book* to find objects of certain lengths using metersticks, skinnies, and bits. They fill in the tables.

Homework

1. Assign *Questions 1–2* in the Homework section of the *m, dm, cm, mm* Activity Pages after Part 1.
2. Assign *Question 3* in the Homework section of the *m, dm, cm, mm* Activity Pages after Part 3.
3. Assign Parts 1 and 2 of the Home Practice.

Assessment

1. Use the *Observational Assessment Record* to document students' abilities to measure length to the nearest mm, cm, dm, and m.
2. Set up a performance assessment task in which students measure specified objects.

Notes:

Answer Key • Lesson 1: m, dm, cm, mm

Student Guide

Questions 1–23 (SG pp. 270–274)

1. Yes
2. No
3. Answers will vary.

4. *A sample class data table follows.

Measurements to the Nearest Meter

Object	Measurement (nearest m)
Height of door	2
Width of classroom	8
Length of classroom	14
Width of chalkboard	5
Length of paper clip	0
Length of pencil	0

---

*Answers and/or discussion are included in the Lesson Guide.

**Answers for all the Home Practice in the *Discovery Assignment Book* are at the end of the unit.

5. A measurement of 0 m tells you the object is less than 0.5 m long. Centimeters or decimeters are more appropriate units.

6. Two possible answers: a pencil and the diameter of a nickel.

7. Two possible answers: The length of a room and the height of a building.

8. *10

9. 10 dm = 1 m; 5 dm = $\frac{1}{2}$ m

10. $\frac{1}{10}$

11. *A sample class data table follows.

Measurements to the Nearest Decimeter

Object	Measurement (nearest dm)
Height of door	22
Width of classroom	84
Length of classroom	137
Width of chalkboard	49
Length of paper clip	0
Length of pencil	1

12. The paper clip is less than 0.5 dm long. Centimeters would give a better measure.

13. Two possible answers: The width of a desk and the length of your arm. (Note: Decimeters are not commonly used in the United States.)

14. 100 bits; explanations will vary.

15. 1 cm

16. *A sample class data table follows.

Measurements to the Nearest Centimeter

Object	Measurement (nearest cm)
Height of door	223
Width of classroom	838
Length of classroom	1372
Width of chalkboard	487
Length of paper clip	3
Length of pencil	14

17. Two possible answers to measure in cm: a calculator and a computer disk. Two possible answers not to measure in cm: distance from school to home and length of side of school building.

18. A possible answer: The thickness of a pencil lead.

19. $\frac{1}{1000}$

20. 10 mm = 1 cm

21. 100 mm = 1 dm; Explanations will vary.

22. *A possible answer: The thickness of a dime.

23. A. 3 metersticks, 4 skinnies, 5 bits
    B. 5 skinnies, 9 bits
    C. 2 metersticks, 7 skinnies
    D. 2 metersticks, 7 bits

Homework (SG p. 275)

Questions 1–3

1. Answers will vary.
2. A.–C. Answers will vary.
3. Answers will vary.

Discovery Assignment Book

**Home Practice (DAB p. 155)

Part 2. Missing Numbers and Big Numbers

Questions 1–3

1. A. $n = 4$ B. $n = 6$ C. $n = 30$
    D. $n = 200$ E. $n = 30$ F. $n = 3$
2. A. 45,089; 45,676; 45,788; 47,998; 48,654; 54,673
    B. 49,000   C. 45,100
3. Answers will vary. Possible answers are:
    A. $600,000 + 30,000 = 630,000$
    B. $2,700,000 + 4,000,000 = 6,700,000$
    C. $400,000 - 100,000 = 300,000$

Class Measurement Tables (DAB p. 163)

*See Figure 3 in the Lesson Guide and *Questions 4, 11* and *16* in the *Student Guide* Answer Key.

Measure Hunt (DAB pp. 165–166)

Answers will vary.

---

*Answers and/or discussion are included in the Lesson Guide.

**Answers for all the Home Practice in the *Discovery Assignment Book* are at the end of the unit.

LESSON GUIDE

Tenths

Estimated Class Sessions: 2–3

Students work with base-ten pieces to build their understanding of tenths using both common fractions and decimal fractions.

Key Content

- Translating between different representations of decimals (concrete, pictorial, verbal, and symbolic).
- Representing decimals using base-ten pieces and number charts.
- Using fractions and decimals to represent the same quantity.
- Reading and writing decimals to the tenths.

Key Vocabulary

common fraction
decimal fraction
denominator
numerator

Daily Practice and Problems: Bits for Lesson 2

E. When Does $\frac{1}{4}$ Matter? (URG p. 15)

1. Might $\frac{1}{4}$ inch be important if you are building a door?

2. Do you think $\frac{1}{4}$ inch is important when you are measuring the distance you can ride on your bike?

3. Give an example when $\frac{1}{4}$ inch is important. Give an example when it's not.

G. Math Fact Practice (URG p. 16)

Solve the problem. Then write the other number sentences in the same fact family.

A. $15 \div 5 =$

B. $27 \div 3 =$

C. $16 \div 2 =$

D. $18 \div 2 =$

E. $21 \div 3 =$

F. $24 \div 3 =$

G. $2 \div 2 =$

DPP Tasks are on page 43. Suggestions for using the DPPs are on page 43.

Curriculum Sequence

Before This Unit

Decimals. Students explored tenths using base-ten pieces in Grade 3 Unit 15. They linked the common fraction $\frac{1}{10}$ to the decimal fraction 0.1.

After This Unit

Fractions. Students will explore common fractions in Grade 4 Unit 12.

Materials List

Print Materials for Students

	Math Facts and Daily Practice and Problems	Activity	Homework
Student Books — Student Guide		*Tenths* Pages 276–282	
Student Books — Discovery Assignment Book		*Tenths Helper* Page 167 and *Grace's Base-Ten Pieces* Page 171	*Exploring Tenths* Pages 169–170 and Home Practice Parts 4 & 5 Page 157
Teacher Resources — Facts Resource Guide	DPP Item 10G		
Teacher Resources — Unit Resource Guide	DPP Items E–H Pages 15–17		

○ *available on Teacher Resource CD*

All Transparency Masters, Blackline Masters, and Assessment Blackline Masters in the Unit Resource Guide are on the Teacher Resource CD.

Supplies for Each Student Pair

meterstick
base-ten pieces (2 packs, 14 flats, 30 skinnies)

Materials for the Teacher

Transparency of *Tenths Helper* Activity Page (Discovery Assignment Book) Page 167
Observational Assessment Record (Unit Resource Guide, Pages 9–10 and Teacher Resource CD)
overhead base-ten pieces

Before the Activity

Make a transparency of the *Tenths Helper* Activity Page. Students will use base-ten pieces during the first and second parts of this lesson. During Part 1, they will use flats and skinnies. During Part 2 they will use packs, flats, and skinnies. Students will also need a meterstick and their *Tenths Helper* Activity Page during Part 1. If necessary, have students work with a partner so that manipulatives can be shared.

Developing the Activity

In Part 1, measurement is used as a model for defining tenths. The base-ten pieces are then redefined for decimals. In Part 2, students continue to explore tenths using the base-ten pieces. Base-ten shorthand is used to record student work. Students explore different ways to express numbers including using the fewest pieces rule. There are several approaches to the material that can be used:

- Work through the *Tenths* Activity Pages in the *Student Guide* with students, using a teacher-led whole class discussion. Supplement the examples in the *Student Guide* with some more of your own.

- Lead the class through activities similar to those in the *Student Guide,* using an overhead projector or chalkboard. Then, assign the *Student Guide* pages to be completed individually or in small groups.

- Assign the *Tenths* Activity Pages in the *Student Guide* for students to work through with a partner or in small groups, and then discuss the pages with the whole class.

Part 1. A New Rule for Base-Ten Pieces

In *Question 1,* students are asked what fraction of the length of a meterstick is 1 skinny. Remind students of the work they did in Lesson 1 when they found that the length of 1 skinny was equal to a decimeter or $\frac{1}{10}$ of a meter. Both the common fraction and the decimal fraction for one tenth are shown. Students review the meaning of the numerator and denominator in common fractions. The meaning of the decimal point is also reviewed.

Content Note

Decimal and Common Fractions. Both $\frac{1}{10}$ and 0.1 are fractions. Fractions like $\frac{1}{10}$ are called "common fractions" or just "fractions." Fractions like 0.1 are called "decimal fractions" or just "decimals."

Tenths

A New Rule for Base-Ten Pieces

 Discuss

In the last lesson, Lee Yah used skinnies to measure to the nearest decimeter. She lined up skinnies along a meterstick. She learned that a skinny is one decimeter long and that a decimeter is one tenth of a meter.

1. A. How many skinnies can you lay along the edge of your meterstick?
   B. The length of one skinny is what fraction of a meterstick?

The fraction for one-tenth can be written as a common fraction ($\frac{1}{10}$). The **denominator** (the number on the bottom) tells us that the meterstick is divided into ten equal parts. The **numerator** (the number on the top) tells us that a skinny is one of these parts.

The fraction for one-tenth can also be written as a decimal fraction (0.1). The decimal point tells us that the numbers to the right of the decimal point are smaller than 1.

$$\frac{1}{10} \begin{array}{l} \text{– numerator} \\ \text{– denominator} \end{array} \qquad \underset{\underset{\text{decimal point}}{\uparrow}}{0.1}$$

2. Place 3 skinnies along the edge of the meterstick.
   A. The length of 3 skinnies is what fraction of a meter?
   B. Write this fraction as a common fraction and as a decimal fraction.

276 **SG · Grade 4 · Unit 10 · Lesson 2**   **Tenths**

Student Guide - Page 276

---

3. Place 5 skinnies along the edge of the meterstick.
   A. The length of 5 skinnies is what fraction of a meter?
   B. Write this fraction as a decimal fraction.
   C. Write this fraction as a common fraction in two different ways.

Doing mathematics is sometimes like playing a game. Just as you cannot play a game without rules, you cannot do mathematics without rules. But, just as people sometimes change game rules, we sometimes change rules in mathematics. And, just as we can still play a game if everyone agrees to the new rules, we can still do mathematics if everyone agrees to the new rules.

Now we are going to change a rule for base-ten pieces. When you worked with base-ten pieces before, usually a bit was one whole. When a bit is the unit, then a skinny is 10 units, a flat is 100 units, and a pack is 1000 units. Now we are going to change which piece is the whole. **For now, a flat will be one whole.**

4. Use skinnies to cover a flat.
   A. How many skinnies did you use?
   B. If a flat is 1 unit, then what fraction is a skinny?

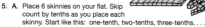

5. A. Place 6 skinnies on your flat. Skip count by tenths as you place each skinny. Start like this: one-tenth, two-tenths, three-tenths. . . .
   B. What fraction of the flat is 6 skinnies?
   C. Write this fraction as a common fraction and a decimal fraction.

Tenths   **SG · Grade 4 · Unit 10 · Lesson 2** 277

Student Guide - Page 277

6. A. Nicholas placed 4 skinnies on his flat. Put 4 skinnies on your flat. Skip count by tenths as you place each skinny.

B. What fraction of the flat is 4 skinnies?

C. Write this fraction as a common fraction and a decimal fraction.

7. A. Linda placed 10 skinnies on her flat. Put 10 skinnies on your flat. Skip count by tenths as you place each skinny.

B. How many tenths is 10 skinnies?

C. Linda noticed that 10 skinnies covered one whole. She recorded this 3 ways: $\frac{10}{10}$, 1, and 1.0. Explain how each of these represents the same number.

You can use the *Tenths Helper* to show how many tenths are in one whole and two wholes.

8. A. Cover your *Tenths Helper* with flats. How many flats did you use?

B. What number does this represent?

9. A. Place 10 skinnies on your *Tenths Helper*. Count by tenths as you place each skinny on the chart.

B. When you are skip counting by tenths, what number comes after 9 tenths? (*Hint*: There is more than one answer to this question.)

C. Continue placing skinnies on your chart. What number will you say as you place the eleventh skinny on the chart? (*Hint*: There is more than one answer to this question.)

D. How many skinnies does it take to fill the *Tenths Helper*?

E. How many tenths are in two wholes?

Tenths

Student Guide - Page 278

Name _____ Date _____

Tenths Helper

Place whole skinnies on this chart to find how many tenths are in one whole and two wholes. Skip count by tenths.

Tenths   DAB · Grade 4 · Unit 10 · Lesson 2 167

Discovery Assignment Book - Page 167

In **Questions 2–3,** students continue to explore decimals using skinnies and a meterstick. In **Question 3,** students place 5 skinnies along the meterstick. This represents five-tenths of a meter. Students are asked to express this fraction as a common fraction in two different ways. They should recognize that $\frac{5}{10}$ is half of the meterstick, so it can also be written $\frac{1}{2}$.

After completing these three questions, students are ready to use base-ten pieces to explore decimals. The first step in using base-ten pieces is to redefine the unit. Redefinition of the unit is a simple but powerful operation. In everyday life, we change our definition of the unit frequently. Depending on our point of view, we think of single eggs or eggs in dozens, of single crayons or boxes of crayons, of individual students or classes of students. Many important fraction and multiplication ideas involve changing perspectives on what "one" is.

A base-ten flat is redefined here to be one whole. A skinny or a pack could also have been defined to be one whole, but they are less convenient for our purposes. Throughout the activity, the unit whole will be a flat.

With a flat as the unit, students can easily model decimals through hundredths. The *Student Guide* pages help students connect the base-ten pieces, base-ten shorthand, words, and symbols for common and decimal fractions.

In **Questions 4–7,** students explore tenths using a flat as one whole. Students skip count by tenths as they build the different numbers. Having students skip count as they place their skinnies on the flat helps them to conceptualize tenths.

Students explore the different ways to write the number 1 in **Question 7.** Review with students that $\frac{10}{10}$ means that you have divided the whole into 10 equal pieces and all ten pieces are being considered and 1.0 means that you have 1 whole and 0 tenths. Both of these are different ways of writing 1 whole.

To complete **Questions 8–11,** students will need their *Tenths Helper* Activity Page in the *Discovery Assignment Book,* as shown in Figure 4. Students use their chart to build 1 whole and 2 wholes using skinnies. Model the use of this chart using the overhead transparency and overhead base-ten pieces. **Question 9A** asks students to place 10 skinnies on the *Tenths Helper* Activity Page, one at a time, counting by tenths. **Question 9B** asks what number comes after nine-tenths. Be sure students understand

that they can say ten-tenths or one (whole).
Question 9C asks students what they will say
when the eleventh skinny is added. Again, students
should understand that they can say either "eleven-
tenths" or "one and one-tenth."

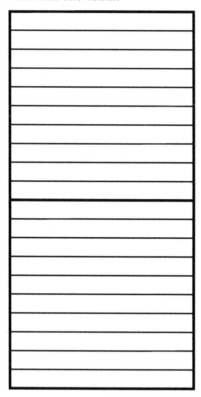

Figure 4: *A Tenths Helper chart*

Part 2. More Tenths

Use base-ten pieces on the overhead to model
Question 12. For *Question 13,* students give the
value of a pack if a flat is one whole. Help students
see that a pack is equal to 10 by counting from one
to ten as you stack 10 flats next to a pack. Base-ten
shorthand is reviewed as a way to record the pieces
used when building a number. See the example
following *Question 13.*

Questions 14–17 can be done independently, in small
groups, or together as a class. In these questions, students use base-ten pieces or base-ten shorthand to
represent numbers. In *Questions 16–17,* students use
base-ten shorthand to show a number between 2 and
3 and between 2.5 and 3. Give students an opportunity to share their numbers and to explain why the
number they chose is appropriate.

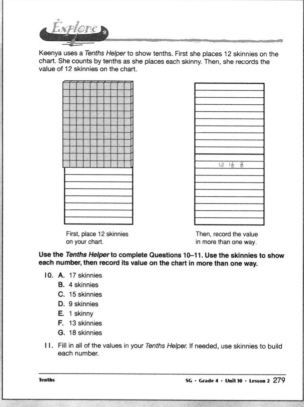

Student Guide - Page 279

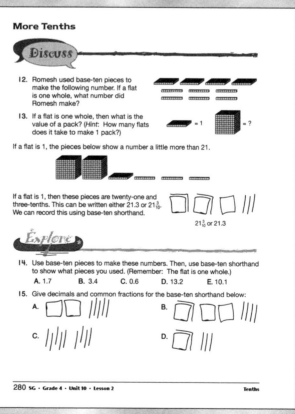

Student Guide - Page 280

Student Guide - Page 281

16. Use base-ten pieces to make a number between 2 and 3. Use base-ten shorthand to show the pieces you used. Then, write your number.

17. Use base-ten pieces to make a number between 2.5 and 3. Use base-ten shorthand to show the pieces you used. Then, write your number.

The Fewest Pieces Rule

 Discuss

The Fewest Pieces Rule says that you should trade ten base-ten pieces for the next size up whenever you can. Ten skinnies should be traded for a flat and ten flats should be traded for a pack. For example, if you had these base-ten pieces:

Using the Fewest Pieces Rule, you should trade ten skinnies for a flat. You would then have these pieces:

 Explore

For Questions 18–20, the flat is one whole. Follow these directions:

    A. Use base-ten shorthand to show how to make the number using the fewest base-ten pieces.

    B. Then, write a decimal for the number.

Make each number first with base-ten pieces. Then, trade to get the fewest pieces. Finally, write the number.

18.

19.

20.

Tenths   SG · Grade 4 · Unit 10 · Lesson 2   281

Discuss the application of the Fewest Pieces Rule with students. Use the base-ten pieces to show that ten skinnies can be traded for a flat and 10 flats can be traded for a pack. Students can then complete *Questions 18–22.*

The *Exploring Tenths* and *Grace's Base-Ten Pieces* Activity Pages in the *Discovery Assignment Book* provide further exploration and practice with decimal concepts.

 Journal Prompt

Compare 1.3 meters and 1.3 with base-ten blocks (A flat is one). How are 1.3 m and 1.3 flats similar? How are they different?

Content Note

Fewest Pieces Rule. While there are usually several ways to show a number using base-ten pieces, there is only one way to show a given number using the fewest base-ten pieces. Every number has a unique "fewest pieces" representation, just as every number has unique representation in our written number system.

Student Guide - Page 282

Showing Numbers in Several Ways

Numbers can be shown in more than one way using base-ten pieces. Suppose a flat is one whole. Then, 2.3 can be shown in these three ways:

21. Use base-ten pieces to make 3.2 in several ways. Use base-ten shorthand to show each way you find. Circle the solution that uses the fewest pieces.

22. Work with a partner to practice making numbers with base-ten pieces and writing them using decimals and common fractions. One person should lay out packs, flats, and skinnies. The other person should write numbers for the pieces. Keep track of your work in a table like this:

Tenths Data Table

Base-Ten Shorthand	Fraction of a Flat	
	Common	Decimal

282 SG · Grade 4 · Unit 10 · Lesson 2   Tenths

Discovery Assignment Book - Page 169

Name _____ Date _____

Exploring Tenths

Use base-ten shorthand to help you answer the following questions.

1. Michael placed 14 skinnies on his *Tenths Helper* chart. Write the number this represents in more than one way.

2. A. Grace wanted to build the number 1.9 on her *Tenths Helper* chart using skinnies. How many skinnies will she need to build this number?

    B. Grace decided to use both flats and skinnies to build this number. How many flats will she need? How many skinnies?

3. Nila built the following number on her *Tenths Helper* chart:

Write this number in more than one way.

4. A. Jackie placed 4 flats on her desk. How many whole units does this represent?

    B. She added 6 skinnies to the 4 flats. What number does 4 flats and 6 skinnies represent?

5. A. Jacob placed 6 skinnies along the edge of a meterstick. The length of 6 skinnies is what fraction of a meter?

    B. Write this fraction as both a decimal fraction and a common fraction.

6. A. Jessie measured the length of a table in her classroom using skinnies. She found the length of the table was 18 skinnies. How many whole meters and how many more tenths does this represent?

    B. Write the length of the table in more than one way.

Tenths   DAB · Grade 4 · Unit 10 · Lesson 2   169

Suggestions for Teaching the Lesson

Math Facts

DPP item G provides practice with fact families.

Homework and Practice

- Assign the *Exploring Tenths* Activity Pages in the *Discovery Assignment Book* for homework.

- DPP items E and F provide practice with measurement. Item H provides computation practice.

- Parts 4 and 5 of the Home Practice can be assigned as homework.

Answers for Parts 4 and 5 of the Home Practice can be found in the Answer Key at the end of this lesson and at the end of this unit.

Name _____ Date _____

7. Use what you know about tenths to complete the table by filling in the missing information. (Remember: A flat is one whole.)

Base-Ten Shorthand	Common Fraction	Decimal Fraction
⫽⫽⫽⫽ ⫽⫽⫽	$\frac{8}{10}$	
		6.7
▱▱▱▱▱▱⫽⫽⫽		
	$23\frac{8}{10}$	
		52.3
▱▱▱▱⫽⫽⫽⫽ ⫽⫽		
▱▱▱▱▱ ⫽⫽		
	$34\frac{8}{10}$	
▱▱▱▱▱▱⫽⫽⫽⫽		

***Discovery Assignment Book* - Page 170**

Daily Practice and Problems: Tasks for Lesson 2

F. Task: Counting Square Units (URG p. 15)

1. How many square millimeters are there in one square centimeter? Use the picture below to help you answer the question.

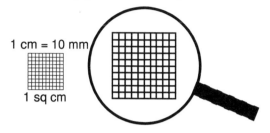

1 cm = 10 mm

1 sq cm

2. How many square centimeters are there in one square meter? It may help if you draw a picture.

H. Task: Addition, Subtraction, and Multiplication Practice (URG p. 17)

Use paper and pencil or mental math to solve the following problems. Be sure to estimate to see if your answers make sense.

1. A. $148 + 779 =$ B. $2090 + 793 =$

   C. $7084 - 557 =$ D. $5386 - 737 =$

   E. $94 \times 7 =$ F. $38 \times 3 =$

   G. $57 \times 2 =$ H. $4068 - 843 =$

   I. $52 \times 9 =$ J. $87 \times 3 =$

2. Explain your strategy for J.

Assessment

- *Grace's Base-Ten Pieces* can be used as a pre-assessment activity to get your students ready for the assessment activity in Lesson 3.

- Homework *Question 7* on the *Exploring Tenths* Activity Pages in the *Discovery Assignment Book* can be used to assess your students' abilities to translate between symbols and physical models for decimals.

- Use the Assessment Indicators as you observe your students working with the base-ten pieces. Use the *Observational Assessment Record* to record students' abilities to translate between concrete, pictorial, and symbolic representations of decimals.

Name _____ Date _____

Grace's Base-Ten Pieces

Use base-ten pieces (packs, flats, and skinnies only). A flat is one whole.

1. If a flat is 1, then what number is a pack?

2. If a flat is 1, then what number is a skinny?

Grace has two base-ten pieces. She might have skinnies, flats, or packs. For example, she might have a skinny and a flat. She might have something else.

3. Find all possible sets of pieces that Grace might have. Use base-ten shorthand to show each set she might have. Write a number for each set.

4. What is the largest number that Grace could possibly have?

5. What is the smallest number that Grace could possibly have?

6. Put the numbers that Grace could have in order from smallest to largest.

Discovery Assignment Book - Page 171

Name _____ Date _____

Part 4   School Supplies

Linda and her brother are buying school supplies. Notebooks are on sale for 39¢ each. Pencils are 4 for $1.00. A set of markers costs $2.98. Folders are 10 for $1.00.

1. Linda needs 3 notebooks, 1 set of markers, 1 folder, and 8 pencils. Estimate the cost of Linda's school supplies. Use number sentences to show your thinking.

2. Linda's brother needs 5 notebooks, 1 set of markers, 3 folders, and 4 pencils. Estimate the cost of his school supplies. Use number sentences to show your thinking.

3. What is the exact cost of each child's supplies? (There is no tax.)

4. What is the difference in price between the two children's supplies? Use a number sentence to show how you solved the problem.

Part 5   Addition, Subtraction, and Multiplication

Solve the following problems using paper and pencil or mental math. Estimate to make sure your answers are reasonable.

1. A. $68 - 49 =$ B. $167 + 67 =$ C. $284 + 238 =$ D. $432 - 197 =$

   E. $47 \times 9 =$ F. $26 \times 7 =$ G. $34 \times 9 =$ H. $23 \times 8 =$

2. Explain your estimation strategy for Question 1F.

3. Explain a possible mental math strategy for Question 1D.

Discovery Assignment Book - Page 157

AT A GLANCE

Math Facts and Daily Practice and Problems

DPP items E and F provide practice with measurement. Bit G provides practice with division facts. Task H provides computation practice.

Part 1. A New Rule for Base-Ten Pieces

1. Lay skinnies along the edge of a meterstick to see that the length of one skinny is one-tenth the length of a meterstick.
2. Write one-tenth as a common fraction. Review the information the numerator and denominator provide. *(Questions 1–3)*
3. Write one-tenth as a decimal fraction. Review the function of the decimal point.
4. Redefine the base-ten pieces. One flat equals one whole.
5. Use skinnies and flats to represent various decimal numbers. *(Questions 4–7)*
6. Use *Questions 8–9* in the *Student Guide* and the *Tenths Helper* Activity Page in the *Discovery Assignment Book* to show how many tenths are in one whole and in two wholes.
7. Students use skinnies to show numbers on the *Tenths Helper* Activity Page. They then write the numbers using common fractions and decimals. *(Questions 10–11)*

Part 2. More Tenths

1. If the flat is one whole, show that the value of a pack is 10. *(Questions 12–13)*
2. Use base-ten shorthand as a way to record the pieces you use to make a number. *(Question 14)*
3. Write a decimal and a common fraction for base-ten shorthand. *(Questions 15–17)*
4. Represent numbers using the fewest pieces rule. *(Questions 18–20)*
5. Represent numbers in more than one way using base-ten pieces. *(Questions 21–22)*
6. Complete *Grace's Base-Ten Pieces* as a pre-assessment activity.

Homework

1. Complete the *Exploring Tenths* Activity Pages in the *Discovery Assignment Book* as homework.
2. Assign Parts 4 and 5 of the Home Practice for homework.

Assessment

Use the *Observational Assessment Record* to document students' abilities to translate between concrete, pictorial, and symbolic representation of decimals.

Notes:

Student Guide

Questions 1–22 (SG pp. 276–282)

1. **A.** *10 skinnies
    B. *$\frac{1}{10}$ or 0.1 m

2. **A.** three-tenths meter
    B. $\frac{3}{10}$ and 0.3

3. **A.** five-tenths meter
    B. 0.5
    C. *$\frac{5}{10}$ m = $\frac{1}{2}$ m

4. **A.** 10 skinnies
    B. $\frac{1}{10}$

5. **B.** six-tenths
    C. $\frac{6}{10}$ and 0.6

6. **B.** four-tenths
    C. $\frac{4}{10}$ and 0.4

7. **B.** 10 tenths
    C. *The ten in the denominator of $\frac{10}{10}$ means that the whole is divided into 10 equal parts and the 10 in the numerator means we are interested in all ten parts. 1 means one whole and 1.0 represents 1 whole and no tenths. All three represent the same number.

8. **A.** 2 flats
    B. 2

9. **B.** *ten-tenths or one whole
    C. *eleven-tenths or one and one-tenth
    D. 20 skinnies
    E. 20 tenths

10. **A.** $\frac{17}{10}$, $1\frac{7}{10}$, or 1.7
    B. $\frac{4}{10}$ or 0.4 (Just writing .4 is acceptable.)
    C. $\frac{15}{10}$, $1\frac{5}{10}$, or 1.5
    D. $\frac{9}{10}$ or 0.9
    E. $\frac{1}{10}$ or 0.1
    F. $\frac{13}{10}$, $1\frac{3}{10}$, or 1.3
    G. $\frac{18}{10}$, $1\frac{8}{10}$, 1.8

11.

0.1		$\frac{1}{10}$
0.2		$\frac{2}{10}$
0.3		$\frac{3}{10}$
0.4		$\frac{4}{10}$
0.5		$\frac{5}{10}$
0.6		$\frac{6}{10}$
0.7		$\frac{7}{10}$
0.8		$\frac{8}{10}$
0.9		$\frac{9}{10}$
1.0		$\frac{10}{10}$
1.1	$1\frac{1}{10}$	$\frac{11}{10}$
1.2	$1\frac{2}{10}$	$\frac{12}{10}$
1.3	$1\frac{3}{10}$	$\frac{13}{10}$
1.4	$1\frac{4}{10}$	$\frac{14}{10}$
1.5	$1\frac{5}{10}$	$\frac{15}{10}$
1.6	$1\frac{6}{10}$	$\frac{16}{10}$
1.7	$1\frac{7}{10}$	$\frac{17}{10}$
1.8	$1\frac{8}{10}$	$\frac{18}{10}$
1.9	$1\frac{9}{10}$	$\frac{19}{10}$
2.0	$1\frac{10}{10}$	$\frac{20}{10}$

12. 4.6

13. *10

14. **A.**

    B.

    C.

    D.

    E.

15. **A.** $2\frac{5}{10}$ and 2.5
    B. $12\frac{4}{10}$ and 12.4
    C. $\frac{9}{10}$ and 0.9
    D. 10.3 and $10\frac{3}{10}$

*Answers and/or discussion are included in the Lesson Guide.

**Answers for all the Home Practice in the *Discovery Assignment Book* are at the end of the unit.

16. Answers will vary

17. Answers will vary.

18. A.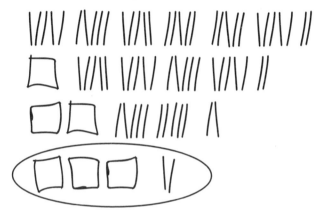

    B. 1 or 1.0

19. A.

    B. 11.7

20. A.

    B. 3.8

21. Answers will vary.

22. Answers will vary.

Discovery Assignment Book

**Home Practice (DAB p. 157)

Part 4. School Supplies

Questions 1–4

1. $3 \times \$0.40 = \$1.20$;
   $\$1.20 + \$3 + \$0.10 + \$2 = \$6.30$

2. $5 \times \$0.40 = \$2$;
   $\$2 + \$3 + \$0.30 + \$1 = \$6.30$

3. Linda: $6.25
   Linda's brother: $6.23

4. $\$6.25 - \$6.23 = \$0.02$ or 2¢

Part 5. Addition, Subtraction, and Multiplication

Questions 1–3

1. A. 19   B. 234
   C. 522   D. 235
   E. 423   F. 182
   G. 306   H. 184

2. Possible strategy: 26×7 is close to 25×7. Skip count by 25s seven times: 25, 50, 75, 100, 125, 150, 175. 26×7 is about 175.

3. Possible strategy: $432 - 197$ is the same as $435 - 200 = 235$.

Exploring Tenths (DAB pp. 169–170)

Questions 1–7

1. $\frac{14}{10}$, $1\frac{4}{10}$, and 1.4

2. A. 19 skinnies
   B. 1 flat and 9 skinnies

3. $\frac{7}{10}$ and 0.7

4. A. 4 wholes
   B. 4.6

5. A. 0.6 m
   B. $\frac{6}{10}$ or 0.6

6. 1 whole meter and 8 tenths (1.8 m)

7.

Base-Ten Shorthand	Common Fraction	Decimal Fraction
‖‖ ‖‖	$\frac{9}{10}$	0.9
⬜⬜⬜⬜⬜ ‖\‖	$6\frac{7}{10}$	6.7
⬜⬜⬜⬜⬜ ‖‖	$33\frac{4}{10}$	33.4
⬜⬜ ⬜⬜⬜ ‖\‖ \	$23\frac{6}{10}$	23.6
⬜⬜⬜⬜⬜⬜ ‖	$52\frac{3}{10}$	52.3
⬜ ⬜ ⬜ ‖‖‖ ‖	$40\frac{7}{10}$	40.7
⬜⬜⬜⬜⬜ \	$5\frac{2}{10}$	5.2
⬜⬜⬜⬜⬜⬜ ‖\	$34\frac{5}{10}$	34.5
⬜⬜⬜⬜⬜ ‖‖	$15\frac{4}{10}$	15.4

---

*Answers and/or discussion are included in the Lesson Guide.

**Answers for all the Home Practice in the *Discovery Assignment Book* are at the end of the unit.

Grace's Base-Ten Pieces (DAB p. 171)

Questions 1–6

1. 10

2. 0.1

3. 20

   11

   10.1

   2

   1.1

   0.2

4. 20

5. 0.2

6. 0.2, 1.1, 2, 10.1, 11, 20

*Answers and/or discussion are included in the Lesson Guide.

**Answers for all the Home Practice in the *Discovery Assignment Book* are at the end of the unit.

LESSON GUIDE 3

Hundredths

Estimated Class Sessions:
3

Students work with base-ten pieces to build their understanding of decimals through hundredths using both common fractions and decimal fractions. An assessment activity concludes the lesson.

Key Content

- Translating between different representations of decimals (concrete, pictorial, verbal, and symbolic).
- Representing decimals using base-ten pieces and number charts.
- Using fractions and decimals to represent the same quantity.
- Reading and writing decimals to the hundredths' place.

Key Vocabulary

denominator
hundredth
numerator

Daily Practice and Problems: Bits for Lesson 3

I. Number Line Decimals (URG p. 17)

The picture below shows a piece of a centimeter ruler enlarged. For each letter, write the decimal that matches.

K. The Price Is Right (URG p. 18)

Fill in the table. Find the largest second factor so that the product of the two numbers is close to the target number without going over the target number. The first has been filled in for you.

Factor 1	Factor 2	Target Number	Left Over
5	7	38	3
3		28	
2		17	
7		25	
6		20	
9		48	
4		13	
5		12	

M. Multiplying with Zeros (URG p. 19)

A. $80 \times 20 =$ B. $40 \times 3 =$

C. $3000 \times 40 =$ D. $20 \times 500 =$

E. $50 \times 30 =$ F. $600 \times 2 =$

G. $0 \times 20 =$ H. $10 \times 60 =$

DPP Tasks and Challenge are on page 56. Suggestions for using the DPPs are on page 56.

Materials List

Print Materials for Students

		Math Facts and Daily Practice and Problems	Activity	Homework	Written Assessment
Student Books	**Student Guide**		*Hundredths* Pages 283–286	*Hundredths* Homework Section Pages 286–287	Student Rubric: *Knowing* Appendix A and Inside Back Cover ⊙
	Discovery Assignment Book		*More Hundredths* Pages 173–174, *Hundredths, Hundredths, Hundredths* Page 175, and *Shorthand and Fractions Table* Page 177	Home Practice Part 3 Page 156	
Teacher Resources	**Facts Resource Guide** ⊙	DPP Items 10K & 10M			
	Unit Resource Guide	DPP Items I–N Pages 17–20 ⊙			*Linda's Base-Ten Pieces* Page 59

⊙   *available on Teacher Resource CD*

All Transparency Masters, Blackline Masters, and Assessment Blackline Masters in the Unit Resource Guide are on the Teacher Resource CD.

Supplies for Each Student Pair

base-ten pieces (2 packs, 14 flats, 30 skinnies, 50 bits)

Materials for the Teacher

Transparency of *Shorthand and Fractions Table* Activity Page (Discovery Assignment Book) Page 177

TIMS Multidimensional Rubric (Teacher Implementation Guide, Assessment section and Teacher Resource CD), optional

Transparency or Poster of Student Rubric: *Knowing* (Teacher Implementation Guide, Assessment section and Teacher Resource CD)

Observational Assessment Record (Unit Resource Guide, Pages 9–10 and Teacher Resource CD)

overhead base-ten pieces, optional

Before the Activity

You will need a transparency of the *Shorthand and Fractions Table* Activity Page in the *Discovery Assignment Book*. This can be used to introduce the game *Hundredths, Hundredths, Hundredths*. It can also provide additional practice for students as needed. Students will need base-ten pieces during this lesson. They will use packs, flats, skinnies, and bits. You may want students to work with a partner so that manipulatives can be shared.

Developing the Activity

There are three parts to this lesson. In the first part, students explore hundredths using a variety of contexts. Students use base-ten shorthand to record the base-ten pieces used to show numbers. You can use one of the following approaches to the first part of this lesson:

* Work through the *Hundredths* Activity Pages in the *Student Guide* with your students in a teacher-led whole-class discussion. Supplement the examples in the *Student Guide* with some more of your own.

* Lead the class through activities similar to those in the *Student Guide*, using an overhead projector or chalkboard. Then, assign the activity pages to be completed with a partner or in small groups.

In the second part of this lesson, students play a game, *Hundredths, Hundredths, Hundredths*. In Part 3, they complete the *Linda's Base-Ten Pieces* Assessment Blackline Master. This assessment can be scored using the Knowing dimension of the *TIMS Multidimensional Rubric*.

Part 1. Exploring Hundredths

This lesson begins with a short vignette in the *Student Guide*. Jackie recognizes that since there are 100 pennies in one dollar, a penny is $\frac{1}{100}$ of a dollar. This can be written as a common fraction ($\frac{1}{100}$) or as a decimal fraction (0.01). In *Question 1,* students are asked what information the **denominator** and the **numerator** give us in a common fraction. Review with students that the denominator tells us how many equal pieces the whole is divided into. In the case of $\frac{1}{100}$, the whole is divided into 100 equal pieces. The numerator tells us how many of the equal parts we are considering. In the case of $\frac{1}{100}$, we are considering one of the equal parts. A penny is one-hundredth of a dollar. Students are then asked to tell what the zeros mean in the decimal fraction 0.01. The zero to the left of the decimal point tells us that there are no whole values. The zero to the right of the decimal point tells us that there are no tenths.

In *Question 2,* students find out what fraction of a dollar 14 pennies represent. They express their answers both as common fractions and as decimal fractions.

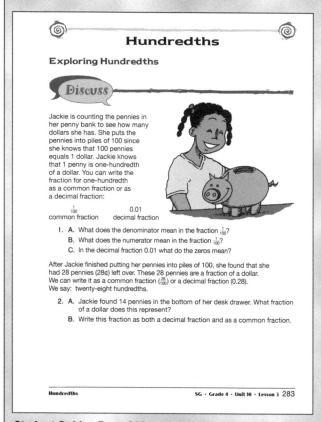

Student Guide - Page 283

100 centimeters = 1 meter

15 cm

3. A. Frank knows that there are 100 centimeters in a meter. That means that the length of one centimeter is 0.01 or $\frac{1}{100}$ of a meter. Frank's pencil is 15 cm long. What fraction of a meter is the length of the pencil?

   B. Write this fraction as both a decimal fraction and as a common fraction.

Irma wanted to use base-ten pieces to show hundredths. She learned in the last lesson that if a flat is 1 whole, then a skinny is 0.1 and a pack is 10.

= 10   = 1   = 0.1

4. Which base-ten piece should Irma use to show one-hundredth? Explain why you chose the piece you did.

5. A. How many hundredths does a skinny represent? Write this number as a common and as a decimal fraction.

   B. How many hundredths does a flat represent? Write this number as a common fraction and as a decimal fraction.

Nicholas used the following base-ten pieces to show a number. If a flat is one whole, then what number do these pieces represent?

These pieces show 3 wholes, 5 tenths, and 7 hundredths. We can write $3\frac{57}{100}$ or 3.57 for this number. We read both $3\frac{57}{100}$ and 3.57 as "Three and fifty-seven hundredths."

6. A. Irma placed the following base-ten pieces on her desk. If a flat is one whole, then what number do these pieces represent?

   B. Write this number as a common fraction and as a decimal fraction.

Student Guide - Page 284

---

7. Mrs. Dewey showed the following base-ten pieces to the class. She asked each student to record the number for these pieces.

   Romesh recorded 5.80 and Jessie recorded 5.8. Explain why both students are correct.

8. Get a handful of mixed skinnies and bits and count them by hundredths. Count the skinnies first (ten-hundredths, twenty-hundredths, thirty-hundredths,...) and then count on for the bits. When you finish, write the number for your handful.

Explore

Tanya used the following base-ten pieces to show the number 3.67.

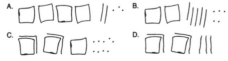

She recorded her work using base-ten shorthand.

9. Use base-ten pieces to make these numbers. Then, use base-ten shorthand to show what pieces you used. A flat is one whole.
   A. 2.34   B. 0.08   C. 0.15   D. 13.42   E. 3.04

10. Give a decimal number and a common fraction for the base-ten shorthand below:

Student Guide - Page 285

In Lesson 1, students learned that since there are 100 centimeters in 1 meter, 1 centimeter is equal to $\frac{1}{100}$ of a meter. In **Question 3,** students are asked what fraction of a meter is 15 centimeters. If students have difficulty answering this question, take out a meterstick and show them what 15 cm looks like.

Students then extend their understanding of decimals to the base-ten pieces. In Lesson 2, a flat was defined as one, a pack as ten, and a skinny as one-tenth. Students are asked to suggest a piece that will show one-hundredth in **Question 4.** They should suggest a bit. If they don't, prompt them by placing a flat on the overhead reminding students that a flat is one whole. Ask:

- *What base-ten piece would we use if we wanted to divide the flat into 10 equal parts?* (A skinny is one-tenth of a flat.)

- *What piece would we use if we wanted to divide the flat into 100 equal parts?* (A bit is one-hundredth of a flat.)

In **Question 5A,** students are asked how many hundredths a skinny represents. Make sure students understand that a skinny is ten-hundredths. Show them that this can be written as 0.10 or as 0.1. It can also be expressed as the common fractions $\frac{1}{10}$ or $\frac{10}{100}$. Help students see that these are all equal by laying 10 bits or ten-hundredths along the side of one skinny or one-tenth. In **Question 5B,** students are also asked how many hundredths a flat represents. Show students that this can be written as $\frac{100}{100}$, as 1, or as 1.00.

In **Questions 6–8,** numbers are represented with base-ten pieces. Students are to give the common fraction and the decimal fraction that name each number. In **Question 6,** students are shown the base-ten pieces representing 2.03, as shown in Figure 5. Make sure students understand that these base-ten pieces represent 2 wholes, zero tenths, and three-hundredths. Provide similar examples for your students if they need more practice.

Figure 5: *Base-ten pieces showing 2.03*

Question 9 reviews the use of base-ten shorthand to record the pieces used to show each number.

Questions 9–16 provide additional practice. Students may work on these with a partner or in small groups. Solutions can then be shared in class as time permits.

Assign the *More Hundredths* Activity Pages in the *Discovery Assignment Book* as homework.

Part 2. *Hundredths, Hundredths, Hundredths*

This game is located in the *Discovery Assignment Book*. Each pair of students will need flats, skinnies, and bits to play the game, as well as a copy of the *Shorthand and Fractions Table* Activity Page in the *Discovery Assignment Book*. Introduce the game using an overhead transparency of the *Shorthand and Fractions Table* Activity Page. Ask two students to demonstrate the game or play a sample game with a student. Begin by reviewing the rules on the *Hundredths, Hundredths, Hundredths* Activity Page. The first player builds a number using base-ten pieces and records his or her number using base-ten shorthand. The second player then records both the common fraction and the decimal fraction for the number and says the number out loud. If the second player does all three things correctly, he or she receives 3 points. If any part of the second player's response is incorrect, he or she will lose a point for that part which is incorrect. For example, if the player says the number correctly, writes the common fraction correctly, but writes the decimal fraction incorrectly, he or she would earn 2 points. Play several rounds during the demonstration game. Make sure to include some examples of numbers that are made without following the fewest pieces rule such as the example at the bottom of the game page, which shows 2.41. Allow time for students to play the game in class.

11. A. Use base-ten pieces to make 0.1 and 0.2.
    B. Use base-ten pieces to make a number more than 0.1 but less than 0.2. Use base-ten shorthand to show the pieces you used. Then, write your number.

12. A. Use base-ten pieces to make 2.5 and 2.6.
    B. Use base-ten pieces to make a number more than 2.5 but less than 2.6. Use base-ten shorthand to show the pieces you used. Then, write your number.

For Questions 13–15, use base-ten shorthand to show how to make the number using the fewest base-ten pieces. Then, write a decimal for the number.

13.
14.
15.

16. If you do not follow the fewest base-ten pieces rule, then the same number can be shown in several ways. Use base-ten pieces to make 0.42 in several ways. Use base-ten shorthand to show each way you find.

Homework

Playing *Hundredths, Hundredths, Hundredths*

Complete these questions after playing *Hundredths, Hundredths, Hundredths*.

1. Lee Yah and Jerome were playing *Hundredths, Hundredths, Hundredths*. Jerome tried to trick Lee Yah by making this number:

Student Guide - Page 286

Name _____ Date _____

Shorthand and Fractions Table

You need base-ten pieces. For this page, a flat is one whole.

Base-Ten Shorthand	Fraction of a Flat	
	Common	Decimal

Discovery Assignment Book - Page 177

Name _____ Date _____

Hundredths, Hundredths, Hundredths

This is a game for two people. You need base-ten pieces (flats, skinnies, and bits). Use the *Shorthand and Fractions Table* to record your work. For this game, a flat is one whole.

Shorthand and Fractions Table

Base-Ten Shorthand	Fraction of a Flat	
	Common	Decimal
	$2\frac{31}{100}$	2.31

To play, the first player makes a number with base-ten pieces and shows it in the table using base-ten shorthand.

Then, the second player must write the fractions for the number and say the number.

The second player scores one point for writing the common fraction correctly, one point for writing the decimal fraction correctly, and one point for saying the number correctly.

Take turns making, writing, and saying numbers.

In this game, you are allowed to be tricky. Can you tell what this number is?

Discovery Assignment Book - Page 175

Part 3. *Linda's Base-Ten Pieces*

The *Linda's Base-Ten Pieces* Assessment Blackline Master assesses students' understanding of decimal notation through hundredths. This activity parallels the *Grace's Base-Ten Pieces* pre-assessment page completed in Lesson 2. In this activity, however, students use packs, flats, skinnies, and bits. Score the assessment using the Knowing dimension of the *TIMS Multidimensional Rubric*. Review the Student Rubric: *Knowing* before beginning the assessment to remind students of your expectations. The following student work has been scored using the Knowing dimension.

Written Work from Student A

Linda's Base-Ten Pieces

You need base-ten pieces (packs, flats, skinnies, and bits.) A flat is one whole.

1. If a flat is 1, then what number is a pack?   10

2. If a flat is **1**, then what number is a skinny?   1/10

3. If a flat is 1, then what number is a bit?   1/100

Linda has two base-ten pieces. She might have bits, skinnies, flats, or packs. For example, she might have two flats. She might have something else.

4. Find all the possible sets of pieces that Linda might have. Use base-ten shorthand to show each set she might have. Write the number for each set.

5. What is the largest number that Linda could possibly have?

6. What is the smallest number that Linda could possibly have?

7. Put the numbers that Linda could have in order from smallest to largest.

Knowing	Level 4	Level 3	Level 2	Level 1
Understands the task's mathematical concepts, their properties and applications…	Completely	Nearly completely	Partially	Not at all
Translates between words, pictures, symbols, tables, graphs, and real situations…	Readily and without errors	With minor errors	With major errors	Not at all
Uses tools (measuring devices, graphs, tables, calculators, etc.) and procedures…	Correctly and efficiently	Correctly or with minor errors	Incorrectly	Not at all
Uses knowledge of the facts of mathematics (geometry definitions, math facts, etc.)…	Correctly	With minor errors	With major errors	Not at all

Student A scored at a level 2 for this task. She correctly identified the value of the pack, skinny, and bit and was able to show 3 possible sets of pieces Linda might have. She did not, however, write a number for any of the three sets. This incomplete answer does not show whether the student has full understanding of the math called for in the problem. The student answered *Questions 5–7* correctly based on her answer to *Question 4,* but, these answers are incomplete. This student used symbols to answer *Questions 5–7* instead of using the common fraction or the decimal fraction. By doing so, she does not show that she understands how to translate between the pictorial and the symbolic representations.

Written Work from Student B

Linda's Base-Ten Pieces

You need base-ten pieces (packs, flats, skinnies, and bits.) A flat is one whole.

1. If a flat is 1, then what number is a pack? *10*

2. If a flat is 1, then what number is a skinny? *.1*

3. If a flat is 1, then what number is a bit? *.01*

Linda has two base-ten pieces. She might have bits, skinnies, flats, or packs. For example, she might have two flats. She might have something else.

4. Find all the possible sets of pieces that Linda might have. Use base-ten shorthand to show each set she might have. Write the number for each set. *[handwritten base-ten shorthand and numbers: .02, .2, .2, 20, .11, .01, 10.1, 11, 1.1, 10.1]*

5. What is the largest number that Linda could possibly have? *20*

6. What is the smallest number that Linda could possibly have? *.02*

7. Put the numbers that Linda could have in order from smallest to largest. *.02, .2, .2, 1.1, 2, 10.01, 10.1, 11, 20*

Knowing	Level 4	Level 3	Level 2	Level 1
Understands the task's mathematical concepts, their properties and applications…	Completely	Nearly completely	Partially	Not at all
Translates between words, pictures, symbols, tables, graphs, and real situations…	Readily and without errors	With minor errors	With major errors	Not at all
Uses tools (measuring devices, graphs, tables, calculators, etc.) and procedures…	Correctly and efficiently	Correctly or with minor errors	Incorrectly	Not at all
Uses knowledge of the facts of mathematics (geometry definitions, math facts, etc.)…	Correctly	With minor errors	With major errors	Not at all

Student B scored at level 4 for this task. It is evident that this student clearly understood each step of this task and how these steps were related to each other. He added the number .21 in *Question 7*. This indicated a minor error translating between the pictures in *Question 4* and the ordering of numbers in *Question 7*. This student found all of the possible sets of pieces that Linda could have. He organized his work by first listing in base-ten shorthand all of the possible doubles. He then listed all the other possibilities systematically. This organization enabled him to make sure he had all of the possible solutions.

Daily Practice and Problems:
Tasks and Challenge for Lesson 3

J. Task: Line Symmetry (URG p. 18)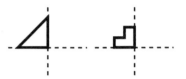

Parts of the pictures below are missing. The dashed lines are lines of symmetry. Copy or trace the pictures on paper and draw in the missing parts.

L. Task: Measuring Angles
  (URG p. 19)

You will need a ruler and a protractor to do these problems.

1. Draw a triangle. Make one angle 38°.

2. Draw a quadrilateral. Make one angle 125°.

3. Draw a hexagon. Make one angle 70°.

N. Challenge: Time (URG p. 20)

1 day = 24 hours

1 hour = 60 minutes

1 minute = 60 seconds

1 week = 7 days

1. 5 hours = ? minutes

2. 4 weeks = ? days

3. 3 days = ? hours

4. $\frac{1}{2}$ hour = ? minutes

5. $\frac{1}{4}$ day = ? hours

6. $\frac{1}{10}$ minute = ? seconds

7. 360 minutes = ? hours

8. 42 days = ? weeks

Suggestions for Teaching the Lesson

Math Facts

DPP Bit K provides practice with division facts by solving problems in which the division does not come out evenly. DPP Bit M provides practice multiplying with multiples of 10.

Homework and Practice

- *More Hundredth*s Activity Pages in the *Discovery Assignment Book* can be assigned after Part 1 of this lesson.

- *Questions 1–7* in the Homework section in the *Student Guide* can be assigned after Part 2 of this lesson.

- For more practice, make up a worksheet using the *Shorthand and Fractions Table*.

- DPP Bit I provides practice reading centimeters to the nearest tenth on a ruler. Tasks J and L are exercises in geometry. J involves symmetry and L involves drawing figures correctly. DPP Challenge N provides practice converting between different units of time.

- Home Practice Part 3 can be assigned as homework for extra practice.

Answers for Part 3 of the Home Practice can be found in the Answer Key at the end of this lesson and at the end of this unit.

Assessment

- Use *Linda's Base-Ten Pieces* Assessment Blackline Master to assess students' understanding of decimal notation.

- Observe students as they work with the base-ten pieces to see if they can readily translate between concrete, pictorial, and symbolic representations of decimals. Record your observations on the *Observational Assessment Record*.

- The journal prompt can be used to assess students' understanding of the relationship between tenths and hundredths.

> ### Journal Prompt
> What are the trading rules for decimals? How many hundredths do you trade for one-tenth? How do decimal trading rules compare with whole number trading rules?

Student Guide - Page 287

For her fractions Lee Yah wrote $\frac{23}{100}$ and 0.023 and said, "Twenty-three hundredths." Lee Yah said she should earn 3 points.

Jerome thought that Lee Yah was wrong, but he couldn't explain why. What do you think?

2. Luis and Ana were playing *Hundredths, Hundredths, Hundredths.* Ana made the following number.

Write the common fraction and the decimal fraction for Ana's number.

3. When it was his turn, Luis made the following number.

Write the common fraction and the decimal fraction for Luis's number.

4. Jessie and Roberto were playing *Hundredths, Hundredths, Hundredths.* Roberto made the following number.

Write the common fraction and the decimal fraction for Roberto's number.

5. When it was Jessie's turn, she wanted to make 6.48. Use base-ten shorthand to show Jessie's number.

6. Roberto wanted to build the number 9.06. Use base-ten shorthand to show what pieces he should use.

7. Jessie wrote nine and six-hundredths like this: 9.6. Explain why this is incorrect.

Hundredths   SG · Grade 4 · Unit 10 · Lesson 3 287

Discovery Assignment Book - Page 156

Name _____ Date _____

Part 3 Decimals

1. Numbers are represented in base-ten shorthand below. The flat is one whole. Label each of the following with its correct number. Then, put the numbers in order from least to greatest.

A.

B.

C.

D.

2. Write a decimal for each of the following. Then, show your decimal using base-ten shorthand. The flat is one whole. Find a number that is:

A. Between 8 and 9   B. Between 4 and 4.5

C. Just a little bigger than 8   D. Between $\frac{1}{2}$ and 2

3. For each of the two problems below, put the measurements in order from shortest to longest.

A. 0.6 m   23 cm   1 dm   0.45 m   55 dm

B. 1.5 m   1 m and 8 dm   1.03 meter   1.24 meter

156 DAB · Grade 4 · Unit 10   USING DECIMALS

Discovery Assignment Book - Page 173

Name _____ Date _____

More Hundredths

Making a Hundredths Chart

Professor Peabody made a hundredths chart. He forgot to fill in some of the chart. Help Professor Peabody by filling in the missing values.

0.01	0.02			0.06					0.1
	0.12		0.15			0.18			
0.21			0.24		0.27				
0.31		0.33			0.36				0.4
				0.45		0.48			
	0.52								
0.61			0.65				0.69	0.7	
	0.73			0.76		0.79			
0.81					0.88			0.9	
0.91		0.93		0.97				1	

Use your completed chart to answer the following questions.

1. A. What number comes after 0.09?

   B. Why is it recorded as 0.1?

2. What number comes after 0.99?

3. Describe any patterns that you see in your hundredths chart.

Hundredths   DAB · Grade 4 · Unit 10 · Lesson 3 173

Discovery Assignment Book - Page 174

Name _____ Date _____

4. Use base-ten shorthand to make these numbers.

A. 19.06

B. 0.68

C. 1.73

D. 44.4

5. Give a decimal fraction and a common fraction for the base-ten shorthand below:

A.

B.

C.

D.

E.

174 DAB · Grade 4 · Unit 10 · Lesson 3   *Hundredths*

AT A GLANCE

Math Facts and Daily Practice and Problems

DPP Bit I provides practice writing decimals using a number line (ruler). Tasks J and L are geometry items. Bits K and M provide math facts practice. For Challenge N, students convert units of time.

Part 1. Exploring Hundredths

1. Introduce the common fraction and the decimal fraction for one-hundredth using the vignette on the *Hundredths* Activity Pages in the *Student Guide*.
2. Use *Questions 1–16* to guide a class discussion.
3. Students use base-ten pieces to represent numbers using hundredths. Students write these numbers as common fractions and decimal fractions. *(Questions 4–8)*
4. Students translate between base-ten pieces, base-ten shorthand, and symbols for numbers to the nearest hundredth. *(Questions 9–16)*

Part 2. *Hundredths, Hundredths, Hundredths*

1. Introduce the game *Hundredths, Hundredths, Hundredths* by playing a demonstration game. Read the rules in the *Discovery Assignment Book*.
2. Students play the game in class. Students can make a recording chart or use the *Shorthand and Fractions Table* in the *Discovery Assignment Book*.

Part 3. *Linda's Base-Ten Pieces*

Review the Student Rubric: *Knowing* and ask students to complete the *Linda's Base-Ten Pieces* Assessment Blackline Master.

Homework

1. Assign the *More Hundredths* Activity Pages in the *Discovery Assignment Book* as homework after Part 1.
2. Assign the Homework section, *Playing Hundredths, Hundredths, Hundredths*, in the *Student Guide* after Part 2.
3. Assign Home Practice Part 3.

Assessment

1. Score the *Linda's Base-Ten Pieces* Assessment Blackline Master using the Knowing dimension of the *TIMS Multidimensional Rubric*.
2. Use the *Observational Assessment Record* to document students' abilities to translate between different representations of decimals.

Notes:

Linda's Base-Ten Pieces

You need base-ten pieces (packs, flats, skinnies, and bits). A flat is one whole.

1. If a flat is 1, then what number is a pack?

2. If a flat is 1, then what number is a skinny?

3. If a flat is 1, then what number is a bit?

Linda has two base-ten pieces. She might have bits, skinnies, flats, or packs. For example, she might have two flats. She might have something else.

4. Find all the possible sets of pieces that Linda might have. Use base-ten shorthand to show each set she might have. Write the number for each set.

5. What is the largest number that Linda could possibly have?

6. What is the smallest number that Linda could possibly have?

7. Put the numbers that Linda could have in order from smallest to largest.

Student Guide

Questions 1–16 (SG pp. 283–286)

1. **A.** *A denominator of 100 means the whole is divided into 100 equal parts.

   B. *A numerator of 1 means we are interested in 1 of the equal parts.

   C. *The 0 to the left of the decimal point in 0.01 means there are no wholes and the 0 to the right of the decimal point means there are no tenths.

2. **A.** fourteen-hundredths

   B. $\frac{14}{100}$ and 0.14 (Writing .14 is acceptable.)

3. **A.** *fifteen-hundredths meter

   B. $\frac{15}{100}$ and 0.15

4. *A bit is used to show one-hundredth because 100 bits make a flat.

5. **A.** *10 hundredths; $\frac{10}{100}$ and 0.10

   B. *100 hundredths; $\frac{100}{100}$ and 1.00 (or 1)

6. **A.** *two and three-hundredths

   B. $2\frac{3}{100}$ and 2.03

7. 5.80 means five wholes, eight tenths, and no hundredths. 5.8 means five wholes and eight tenths and no hundredths is implied.

8. Answers will vary.

9. **A.**

   B. : : : ˙ ˙

   C. | ˙ ˙ ˙ ˙ ˙

   D.

   E. ⬜⬜⬜ ˙ ˙ ˙ ˙

10. **A.** 4.23 and $4\frac{23}{100}$ **B.** 2.57 and $2\frac{57}{100}$
    C. 21.09 and $21\frac{9}{100}$ **D.** 20.3 and $20\frac{3}{10}$

11. **A.** 1 and 11

    B. Answers will vary.

12. **A.**  and

    B. Answers will vary.

13. 1.83

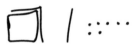

14. 2.41

15. 10.17

16. Answers will vary.

Homework (SG pp. 286–287)

Questions 1–7

1. Lee Yah is wrong because the 0 in the tenths' place in 0.023 means that there are no tenths. Since the twenty bits can be traded for two skinnies with 3 bits (3 hundredths) left over, the number should be written 0.23.

2. $2\frac{52}{100}$ and 2.52

3. $2\frac{91}{100}$ and 2.91

4. $\frac{54}{100}$ and 0.54

5.

6.

7. 9.6 means 9 wholes and 6 tenths, not 9 wholes and 6 hundredths.

*Answers and/or discussion are included in the Lesson Guide.

**Answers for all the Home Practice in the *Discovery Assignment Book* are at the end of the unit.

Discovery Assignment Book

**Home Practice (DAB p. 156)

Part 3. Decimals

Questions 1–3

I. **A.** 3.3   **B.** 3.6

   C. 3.03   **D.** 4.4

                            3.03; 3.3; 3.6; 4.4

2. Answers will vary.

3. **A.** 1 dm, 23 cm, 0.45 m, 0.6 m, 55 dm

   B. 1.03 m, 1.24 m, 1.5 m, 1 m and 8 dm

More Hundredths (DAB pp. 173–174)

Questions 1–5

I. **A.** 0.1

   B. 0.1 means there is one-tenth or 1 skinny. Since 1 skinny is equal to 10 bits, one-tenth is equal to ten-hundredths (0.1 = 0.10). Note that in the decimal 0.10, the one means there is one-tenth and the second zero means there are no hundredths.

2. 1.00 or 1

3. Answers will vary.

4. **A.**

   B.

   C.

   D.

5. **A.** $24\frac{37}{100}$ and 24.37   **B.** $13\frac{9}{100}$ and 13.09

   C. $30\frac{3}{100}$ and 30.03   **D.** $5\frac{3}{10}$ and 5.3

   E. $22\frac{22}{100}$ and 22.22

Unit Resource Guide

Linda's Base-Ten Pieces (URG p. 59)

Questions 1–7

I. 10

2. 0.1

3. 0.01

4.

 20

 11

 10.1

 10.01

 2

                1.1

                1.01

                0.2

                0.11

                0.02

5. 20

6. 0.02

7. 0.02, 0.11, 0.2, 1.01, 1.1, 2, 10.01, 10.1, 11, 20

---

*Answers and/or discussion are included in the Lesson Guide.

**Answers for all the Home Practice in the *Discovery Assignment Book* are at the end of the unit.

Daily Practice and Problems:
Bits for Lesson 4

0. Skip Counting (URG p. 20)

1. Skip count by dimes to $2.00.
   Start like this: $0.10, $0.20, $0.30 . . .

2. Skip count by tenths to 2.
   Start like this: 0.1, 0.2, 0.3 . . .

3. Skip count by quarters to $5.00.
   Start like this: $0.25, $0.50, $0.75 . . .

4. Skip count by 0.25 (twenty-five
   hundredths) to 5. Start like this:
   0.25, 0.50, 0.75 . . .

Q. More Fact Families for × and ÷
   (URG p. 22)

The following four facts are in the same
fact family.

$4 \times 3 = 12$ $3 \times 4 = 12$

$12 \div 3 = 4$ $12 \div 4 = 3$

Solve each pair of related number sentences. Then,
give two other facts that are in the same fact family.

A. $7 \times 2 = ?$ and $14 \div 7 = ?$

B. $2 \times 3 = ?$ and $6 \div 2 = ?$

C. $3 \times 8 = ?$ and $24 \div 3 = ?$

D. $6 \times 3 = ?$ and $18 \div 3 = ?$

E. $4 \times 2 = ?$ and $8 \div 4 = ?$

F. $3 \times 8 = ?$ and $24 \div 8 = ?$

G. $3 \times 1 = ?$ and $3 \div 1 = ?$

S. Write a Decimal (URG p. 23)

1. Write a decimal:

   A. between 7 and 8

   B. between 1 and 2

   C. just a little bigger than 4

   D. just a little less than 2

   E. between $\frac{1}{2}$ and 0.8

   F. between 5 and 5.5

2. Explain your strategy for E.

DPP Tasks are on page 71. Suggestions for using the
DPPs are on page 71.

LESSON GUIDE 4
Downhill Racer

Estimated
Class
Sessions:
4

Students roll cars down ramps to investigate
the relationship between the height of the
ramp and the distance a car travels after
it has left that ramp. This lab provides a
context for students to use decimals and measure
length in meters.

Key Content

- Identifying fixed variables in an experiment.
- Measuring length to the nearest hundredth
  of a meter.
- Collecting, organizing, graphing, and
  analyzing data.
- Using patterns in graphs to make predictions.
- Comparing and ordering decimals.

Key Vocabulary

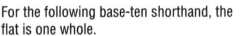

extrapolate   manipulated variable
fixed variables   responding variable
interpolate   variables

U. Smallest, Largest, and In-Between
   (URG p. 24)

For the following base-ten shorthand, the
flat is one whole.

1. ☐☐☐ ////

2. ☐☐☐☐ ///

3. ☐ // ☐ // ☐ // ☐

4. ☐☐ /// ☐☐

A. Which is the smallest?

B. Which is the largest?

C. Which are equal?

D. Write numbers for each and put
    them in order from smallest to
    largest. (The flat is one whole.)

Materials List

Print Materials for Students

	Math Facts and Daily Practice and Problems	Lab	Homework	Written Assessment
Student Book — Student Guide		*Downhill Racer* Pages 288–294	*Downhill Racer* Homework Section Page 295	
Teacher Resources — Facts Resource Guide ⊙	DPP Item 10Q			
Unit Resource Guide ⊙	DPP Items O–V Pages 20–24			*Roberto's Data* Pages 74–75
Generic Section ⊙		*Centimeter Graph Paper*, at least 3 per student and *Three-trial Data Table*, 1 per student		

⊙ available on Teacher Resource CD

All Transparency Masters, Blackline Masters, and Assessment Blackline Masters in the Unit Resource Guide are on the Teacher Resource CD.

Supplies for Each Group

incline (wood or metal, at least 50 cm long)
roller skate, pinewood derby car, or other toy car
metersticks (two or three)
blocks or books (four or five, all the same size)
masking tape
calculators

Materials for the Teacher

Transparency of *Centimeter Graph Paper* (Unit Resource Guide, Generic Section)
Observational Assessment Record (Unit Resource Guide, Pages 9–10 and Teacher Resource CD)
Individual Assessment Record Sheet (Teacher Implementation Guide, Assessment section and Teacher Resource CD)

Curriculum Sequence

Before This Unit

Best-fit Lines. Students used best-fit lines to make predictions in Unit 5 Lesson 1 *Predictions from Graphs* and Lesson 4 *Bouncing Ball* lab. They also used best-fit lines in the lab *Volume vs. Number* in Unit 8.

Medians. Students used medians to average data collected in labs in Grades 1, 2, and 3. The median was reviewed in Unit 1 Lesson 3 *An Average Activity.* Students used averages in previous fourth-grade labs and activities. (The mean was introduced in Unit 5.)

TIMS Laboratory Method. Students used the TIMS Laboratory Method to collect, organize, graph, and analyze data in Units 1, 2, 5, and 8.

After This Unit

Best-fit Lines. Students will use graphs to make predictions in the labs *Plant Growth* and *Taste of TIMS* in Unit 15 and *Area vs. Length* in Unit 16. They will need to decide when it is appropriate to draw a best-fit line.

Medians. Students will continue to average data in labs and activities throughout the year. (See Units 13 and 15 for specific examples.)

TIMS Laboratory Method. Students will encounter labs in Units 14, 15, and 16.

Before the Lab

Ask students to bring toy cars and roller skates (not in-line skates) to class for this lab. All cars should be tested prior to beginning the lab. The lab requires cars that roll straight for consistent distances. The floor where the cars are rolled should be a level surface without cracks or bumps.

A primary goal of this lab is for students to practice controlling variables. Many things can affect the distance the cars roll: type of car, height of the ramp, exact location of the ramp in the room (since some parts of the floor may be bumpier than other parts), position of the starting line on the ramp, how the car is released, and "accidents" (e.g., bumping the side of the ramp). Of all these variables, only the ramp height is allowed to change; the others must stay fixed.

For this reason and to help students stay focused during the lab, they should be familiar with the equipment before they begin. The following steps can help:

1. Students bring in cars from home several days before the activity.

2. Set up a ramp area (or two) with inclines, blocks, or books, and metersticks.

3. Let the children play with the cars informally during free time for a few days. You might suggest a "roll-off" during recess.

4. Ask the students to identify "good rollers." A good roller will roll straight for about 2 meters or more.

> ## TIMS Tip
>
> If a large area such as the gym or playground is not available or if you do not have access to a ramp for each group, then you can set up a smaller number of ramps. Students can draw their pictures or work on DPP items while they wait for their group's chance to collect data.

5. Discuss *"What variables affect how far a car rolls?"*

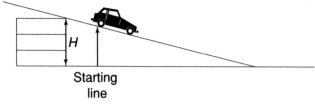

Figure 6: *Ramp setup*

DPP item O provides practice skip counting by 0.1s and 0.25s. This item will prepare students for scaling their graphs.

Developing the Lab

This lab uses the TIMS Laboratory Method: beginning the investigation, gathering and organizing the data, graphing the data, and analyzing the results.

Part 1. Beginning the Investigation

One way to introduce the lab is to set up two ramps, one held up by two blocks or books, the other held up by four blocks or books. Show students the car which will be rolled down both ramps.

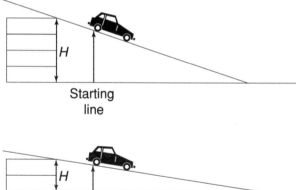

Figure 7: *Racing areas with different heights*

Ask:

- *What is the same in these two racing areas?* (The type of ramp and the type of car.)

- *What is different?* (One ramp is higher.)

- *If I release the car on each ramp, how far will the car roll on the floor? Which ramp will make the car roll farther?* The role of variables like the starting point, the kind of car, the manner of release, and so on, can be highlighted by manipulating this setup.

TIMS Tip

If at all possible, schedule data collection for a day with time for an extended class when students can gather their initial data and make and check predictions *(Questions 9–11)*, without having to set up again. This way all the variables included in the ramp setup will stay fixed, so students' predictions will be much more reliable. If this is not possible, each group should label their cars and ramps. Starting points for the cars and the point at which the blocks or books touch the ramp should be marked on each ramp.

Downhill Racer

Jackie and her brother Derrick want to play with their toy cars. They set up a ramp using the steps in front of their apartment building and a piece of thick plywood.

Jackie suggested using a meterstick to find how far each car traveled. Derrick wondered, "Will the cars roll different distances if we put the ramp on different steps?"

I think the cars will roll farther with the ramp on a higher step.

Downhill Racer

Student Guide - Page 288

---

1. Do you think a car will roll farther when the ramp is set up on a higher step? Explain why you think so.

Jackie and Derrick did an experiment to find out how far each car rolled when the ramp was put on steps of different heights. First, they talked about how to be sure that the experiment was fair. Derrick suggested that the starting line on the ramp should stay the same.

2. What other variables should not change during the experiment? Why?

3. Jackie and Derrick decided to run three trials for each different height. Why was this a good idea?

Use the TIMS Laboratory Method to do an experiment like Jackie and Derrick's. Use a car and a ramp to study the relationship between the height of the ramp (H) and the distance your car will roll on the ground (D).

Use blocks or books to change the height of the ramp. The height (H) is the height of the blocks (or books). The blocks should touch the ramp at the same place for the entire experiment. The distance (D) should be measured from the bottom of the ramp to the back wheels of the car.

4. What is the manipulated variable?

5. What is the responding variable?

Draw a picture of the lab. Be sure to show the two main variables, Height (H) and Distance (D). Also show the length of your ramp and where your starting line is.

6. Later, you will make and check predictions about how far your car rolls. Unless you are careful now, you may not be able to check your predictions later. Write a paragraph that describes exactly how you set up your lab, so that later you can set it up again in exactly the same way. (*Hint:* Look at your answer to Question 2.)

Downhill Racer

Student Guide - Page 289

Introduce the lab using the *Downhill Racer* Lab Pages in the *Student Guide.* Explain that instead of using the steps from Jackie's apartment building, the class will use books or blocks to investigate the relationship between the height of a ramp and how far a car rolls.

To investigate the effect changing the height has on the distance the car rolls, all other variables involved in the experiment should be held fixed. In planning the experiment, students should discuss these variables (*Question 2*):

- car (Each group should use the same car throughout.)

- type of floor (Each ramp should remain in the same location throughout.)

- method of releasing the car (The back wheels should be placed on the starting line and the car should be released gently without being pushed. Do not use spring-loaded cars.)

- position of the stack of blocks or books where the height (*H*) is measured (at the same place under the ramp)

- how far the starting line is from the bottom of the ramp (Before students collect the data, the starting line can be adjusted so that the car rolls a reasonable amount. Then, it should be marked with tape.)

- how the distance rolled (*D*) is measured (from the bottom of the ramp to the back wheel of the car)

Manipulated and Responding Variables. The **manipulated variable** (*Question 4*) is the variable with values we select at the beginning of the experiment. In this lab it is the height of the ramp (*H*). Either you select the heights or let the students select them. In any case, the values should be chosen so that the cars will roll a reasonable distance, yet not roll too far. Try out different heights using different numbers of books or blocks that are the same thickness. The values should be well-spaced for easy graphing and preferably in some proportional pattern. Values like *H* = 4 cm, 8 cm, 12 cm or *H* = 4 cm, 16 cm, 24 cm work well. For example, you could use 1, 2, and 4 geography books or 2, 4, and 6 spelling books to get the desired heights in cm.

The **responding variable** (*Question 5*) is the variable with values we find during the experiment. Here, it is the distance the car rolls on the floor (*D*). After the car stops, students should measure the distance from the bottom edge of the incline to the rear wheels of the car, as shown in Figure 8. This distance should be measured to the nearest hundredth of a meter and expressed using decimals.

Pictures. After you have discussed the lab and students understand the procedures, they draw pictures of the investigation. Emphasize that a good picture shows the equipment, identifies the variables, and communicates the procedures. Students' pictures can help you judge who is ready to go on to the next phase—gathering data. The picture in Figure 9 shows the experimental setup and the two main variables labeled *H* and *D*. However, it does not clearly show the method for measuring the distance—from the end of the ramp to the rear wheels.

Part 2. Gathering and Organizing the Data

Multiple Trials. Discuss how many trials should be made for each height. The data table shown in the *Student Guide* allows for three trials, but a different number could be made if you prefer. The important point is that there be multiple trials.

Discuss bad trials, as when the car rolls off the side of the ramp. Ask whether including such trials would be fair. Help students understand why these trials should be discarded. All measurements for trials with the same height should have distances that are close to one another.

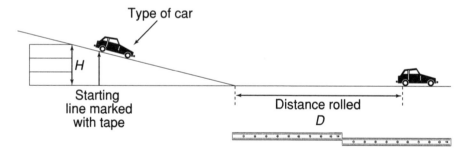

7. **A.** Work with your group to do the experiment.
   - Discuss what values for the height (*H*) you will use.
   - Measure the height in centimeters.
   - Measure the distance (*D*) the car rolls to the nearest hundredth of a meter. Use decimals to record your measurements of this distance.
   - Do three trials for each height. Average the three distances for each height by finding the median distance.
   - Keep track of your data in a table like this one:

H Ramp Height (in cm)	*D* Distance Rolled (in m)			
	Trial 1	Trial 2	Trial 3	Average

   B. Why is it a good idea to find the average distance?

   Graph

8. **A.** Plot your data points on *Centimeter Graph Paper.* Put the manipulated variable on the horizontal axis and the responding variable on the vertical axis. Remember to title your graph, label axes, and record units. Before you scale your axes, discuss with your group how much room you need on your graph for extrapolation. (*Hint:* Look at Questions 9–12.)
   B. Look at your points on the graph. Do the points lie close to a straight line? If so, use a ruler to fit a line to the points. Extend the line in both directions.

290 SG · Grade 4 · Unit 10 · Lesson 4   **Downhill Racer**

Student Guide - Page 290

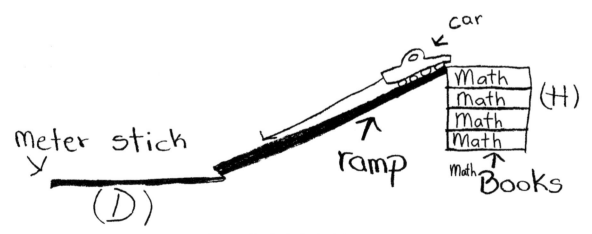

Figure 8: *Measuring the height (H) and the distance (D)*

Figure 9: *A student picture*

TIMS Tip

Students should be in groups of three or four. Each member might have a job: a Roller, a Measurer, a Recorder, and a Fairness Officer who checks to see that variables are held fixed.

H Ramp Height (in cm)	D Distance Rolled (in m)			
	Trial 1	Trial 2	Trial 3	Average
4 cm	1.23 m	1.25 m	1.23 m	1.23 m
8 cm	2.56 m	2.52 m	2.54 m	2.54 m
12 cm	3.67 m	3.71 m	3.64 m	3.67 m

Figure 10: *A student data table (averages are medians)*

Answer the following questions using your graph:

9. If the height of the ramp were 10 cm,
   A. How far would your car roll? H = 10 cm; Predicted D = ?
   B. Did you interpolate or extrapolate?
   C. Check your prediction. H = 10 cm; Actual D = ?
   D. Was your predicted distance close to the actual distance?

10. If the height of the ramp were 16 cm,
    A. How far would your car roll? H = 16 cm; Predicted D = ?
    B. Did you interpolate or extrapolate?
    C. Check your prediction. H = 16 cm; Actual D = ?
    D. Was your predicted distance close to the actual distance?

11. A. Predict how high the ramp should be if you want the car to roll 1.5 m. Explain how you found your answer.
    B. Check your prediction. How close did your car roll to 1.5 m?

12. Imagine doing the experiment again, this time letting the car go from a lower starting point on the ramp. Would your new line look like Line A or Line B? Explain why you think so.

13. Sometimes knowing one variable helps in predicting another.
    A. Does knowing the height of the ramp (H) help you predict what the distance rolled (D) will be?
    B. Does knowing the distance rolled (D) help you predict what the height of the ramp (H) was?
    C. As the height of the ramp (H) increases, how does the distance (D) change?

Downhill Racer   SG · Grade 4 · Unit 10 · Lesson 4 **291**

Student Guide - Page 291

Setting up the Ramps. Ideally, the cars should roll at least two meters at the maximum height, so students should try a variety of starting points before they begin to gather their data. They may notice that if they start at the top of the ramp, the car rolls too far or takes a bad roll. Students should make a mark on the ramp with a piece of masking tape so that the starting point is the same each time. *Question 6* asks students to describe their setups as precisely as possible so that later they can check their predictions using exactly the same setups.

Once all the trials are done, the students find the average distance rolled. They should use the median since they have not yet calculated with decimals. Finding the median also provides a good opportunity for them to order decimals. In *Question 7B,* they are asked why taking an average is a good idea. So much can go wrong in any experiment that repeated measurements are crucial. Due to small errors, we average the data to get the most accurate result; averaging reduces the effect of random errors we cannot control.

Part 3. Graphing the Data and Analyzing the Results

Deciding how much room to leave for extrapolation is not easy. No exact rule can be given, only that *some* room should be allowed. Questions later in the lab ask about ramp heights up to 16 cm. Numbering the horizontal axis to 30 cm should suffice. Numbering the vertical axis will depend on the longest distance available for the car to roll. Students may need help scaling the vertical axis using decimals. See Figure 11. (DPP Item O will prepare students for scaling their graphs.)

Questions 9–11 explore interpolation, extrapolation, and predicting. Students should mark their predictions on the graph as shown in Figure 11. They should then check their predictions experimentally. For students' predictions to be close, the experimental setups must be the same—all variables must be held fixed except the height of the ramp.

📓 Journal Prompt

• Why is it better to measure the distance to the nearest hundredth of a meter instead of to the nearest whole meter, or to the nearest tenth of a meter, or to the nearest thousandth of a meter?

• Write a story about a team that didn't control an important variable in *Downhill Racer.* Tell what they failed to control and what happened.

In *Questions 9D, 10D,* and *11B,* ask if students' predictions are close. Help students decide if their predictions are close. (Even students who completed Unit 6 Lesson 5 need not use the 10% standard in this lab because they have not had experience with decimal computation.) Students should understand that "closeness" is relative. The difference between predicted distances and actual measurements can be greater for longer distances than shorter distances. For example, a prediction of 5 m can be considered close if the actual measurement is within 0.5 m. However, a predicted distance of 1 m would not be considered close if the actual distance the car rolled was 0.5 m or 1.5 m, but it would be if the rolling distance were between 0.9 m and 1.1 m.

For *Question 11B,* you might ask a limited number of students to check their predictions.

In *Question 12,* one of the fixed variables is changed: the starting point on the ramp is lowered. The car does not build up as much speed and therefore will not roll as far. The new graph would look like Line A.

Content Note
Why Does the Car Roll and Stop? It is gravity that pulls the car down the incline and friction that stops it. If the release point is lowered, gravity does not act for as long a time and the car will not go as far.

Part 4. Explore Questions
Questions 14–19 review several concepts developed in Grade 4. In the context of a slight variation on the *Downhill Racer* lab, students identify different types of variables, graph data, make predictions when changing one variable, and find both kinds of averages. Students may work on the problems individually or in groups, as class work or as homework. Students will need calculators and *Centimeter Graph Paper.*

The focus of the problems is an experiment similar to *Downhill Racer* but in which the height of the ramp stays the same and the starting point on the ramp changes. *Question 14* requires students to use their knowledge of variables to identify manipulated, responding, and fixed variables and to distinguish between numerical and categorical variables.

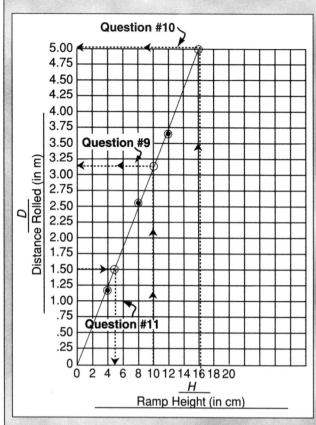

Figure 11: *Predictions on student's graph*

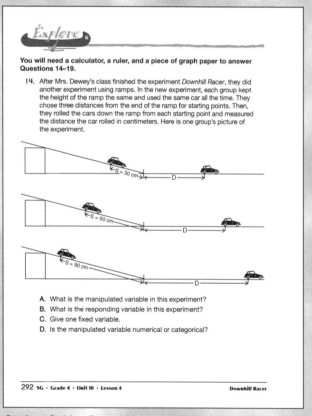

Student Guide - Page 292

15. John's group rolled its car down the ramp three times from the starting point that was 60 cm from the end of the ramp. Here are the distances the car rolled for three trials: 83 cm, 84 cm, and 89 cm.
   A. Find the mean distance for these trials. Give your answer to the nearest centimeter.
   B. Find the median distance.

16. Nila's group chose to do four trials. Here are the distances the car rolled from a starting point that was 120 cm from the end of the ramp: 189 cm, 177 cm, 186 cm, and 188 cm.
   A. Find the mean distance for these trials.
   B. Find the median distance. Give your answer to the nearest centimeter.

17. Here is Shannon's data. Make a graph of the data.

Shannon's Data

H Starting Distance From End of Ramp (in cm)	D Distance Rolled (in cm)			
	Trial 1	Trial 2	Trial 3	Average
30	48	47	47	47
60	87	84	86	86
90	144	142	145	144

Downhill Racer — SG · Grade 4 · Unit 10 · Lesson 4 **293**

Compare the variables in this situation with those in the lab the students just completed. Ask:

- *What was the manipulated variable in the Downhill Racer lab?* (Height of the incline)
- *What kind of a variable is height in **Question 14?*** (Fixed)
- *What is the manipulated variable in **Question 14?*** (Starting point of the car)
- *What kind of variable was the starting point in the Downhill Racer lab?* (Fixed)
- *What are some other variables that could be investigated by making them the manipulated variable?* (Students may suggest the size of car, type of wheels on the car, floor surface, or surface of the incline. Have students make conjectures about what they would find out by making any one of these variables the manipulated variable.)

Questions 15 and *16* ask students to find both medians and means of a given set of data and to give their answers to the nearest centimeter. Students graph a set of data and use the graph to make predictions using interpolation and extrapolation in *Questions 17–19*.

---

18. A. Use your graph to predict the distance the car will roll if Shannon uses the same lab setup and she starts to roll the car down the ramp 45 cm from the end of the ramp.
   B. Did you use interpolation or extrapolation to find your answer?

19. A. Use your graph to predict the distance the car will roll if Shannon uses the same lab setup and she starts to roll the car down the ramp 120 cm from the end of the ramp.
   B. Did you use interpolation or extrapolation to find your answer?

294 SG · Grade 4 · Unit 10 · Lesson 4 — Downhill Racer

Homework

Miss Take made the following graph for Roberto's data. She has made many mistakes. How many can you find? Write a letter to Miss Take explaining as many errors as you can find.

Name: _Miss Take_

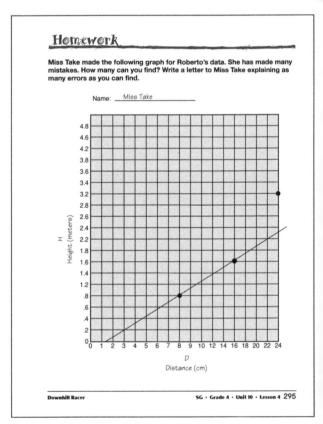

Downhill Racer — SG · Grade 4 · Unit 10 · Lesson 4 **295**

Suggestions for Teaching the Lesson

Math Facts

DPP Bit Q provides practice with division facts using fact families.

Homework and Practice

- Assign some or all of *Questions 14–19* in the Explore section of the *Student Guide* for homework. These problems review the concepts and procedures developed in this lab and previous labs. (Students will need a piece of *Centimeter Graph Paper*.)

- DPP items O and P provide practice skip counting with decimals. Items R, S, and U develop number sense with decimals. Items T and V provide practice with metric measurement.

Daily Practice and Problems: Tasks for Lesson 4

P. Task: Skip Counting by Tenths and Hundredths (URG p. 21)

1. Use a calculator to skip count by tenths. Skip count by tenths from 0 to 2.

   Press: `0` `+` `.` `1` `=` `=` `=`

   Say the numbers quietly to yourself.

2. Skip count by hundredths from 0 to one-tenth.

   Press: `0` `+` `.` `0` `1` `=` `=`

   Say the numbers quietly to yourself.

3. Skip count by tenths from 5 to 7.

   Press: `5` `+` `.` `1` `=` `=` `=`

   Say the numbers quietly to yourself.

4. Skip count by hundredths from 2 to 2.1.

   Press: `2` `+` `.` `0` `1` `=` `=`

   Say the numbers quietly to yourself.

R. Task: Ordering Decimals (URG p. 22)

1. Draw each of the following numbers in base-ten shorthand. The flat is one whole. Then, put the numbers in order from smallest to largest:

   0.4   0.39   0.41   0.5   1.00

2. Draw each of the following numbers in base-ten shorthand. The flat is one whole. Then, put these numbers in order from smallest to largest:

   0.09   0.8   1.0   0.27   0.01

T. Task: Which Length Is Longer? (URG p. 23)

1. Use a meterstick to help you answer the following.

   (Bits and skinnies might help, too. Remember, one bit is one centimeter long. One skinny is 10 cm or 1 decimeter long.) Which is longer:

   A. 2 cm or 11 mm?

   B. 32 mm or 3 cm?

   C. 5 dm or 45 cm?

   D. 2 m or 180 cm?

   E. 3 dm or 300 mm?

   F. 87 cm or 8 dm?

2. Choose one of the questions and explain your strategy for solving it.

V. Task: Metric Conversions (URG p. 24)

Change each of these lengths to meters.
(*Hint:* Think of metersticks, skinnies, and bits.)

   A. 327 cm   B. 405 cm

   C. 5 cm   D. 87 cm

   E. 10 dm   F. 24 dm

Change each of these lengths to centimeters.

   G. 1.1 m   H. 1.01 m

   I. 4 dm   J. 4.1 dm

   K. 3.27 m   L. 0.4 dm

Suggestions for Teaching the Lesson (continued)

- In the Homework section students are asked to find errors in Miss Take's graph of Roberto's data. Accordingly, this homework must be assigned after students have completed the *Roberto's Data* Assessment Blackline Master. Sample student work is shown in Figure 12.

  Notice that Ana identified errors on the axes, both in scaling and labeling. She also recognized that the data points were not plotted correctly. Miss Take did not accurately determine where the average distances of 0.95 m, 1.79 m, and 2.97 lie along the vertical axis. Ana also demonstrated knowledge of how to draw a best-fit line through a set of data points.

Assessment

- In *Roberto's Data* Assessment Blackline Master students are given sample data for *Downhill Racer* to graph and analyze. This exercise can be used to assess how well students can measure and graph decimals and how well they understand the meaning of the lab *Downhill Racer*. Students will need a copy of *Centimeter Graph Paper* to complete the assessment.

- Use the *Observational Assessment Record* to document students' progress in conducting experiments using the TIMS Laboratory Method. Note how well students collect data. In particular, note how well they keep appropriate variables fixed.

- Transfer information from the Unit 10 *Observational Assessment Record* to students' *Individual Assessment Record Sheets*.

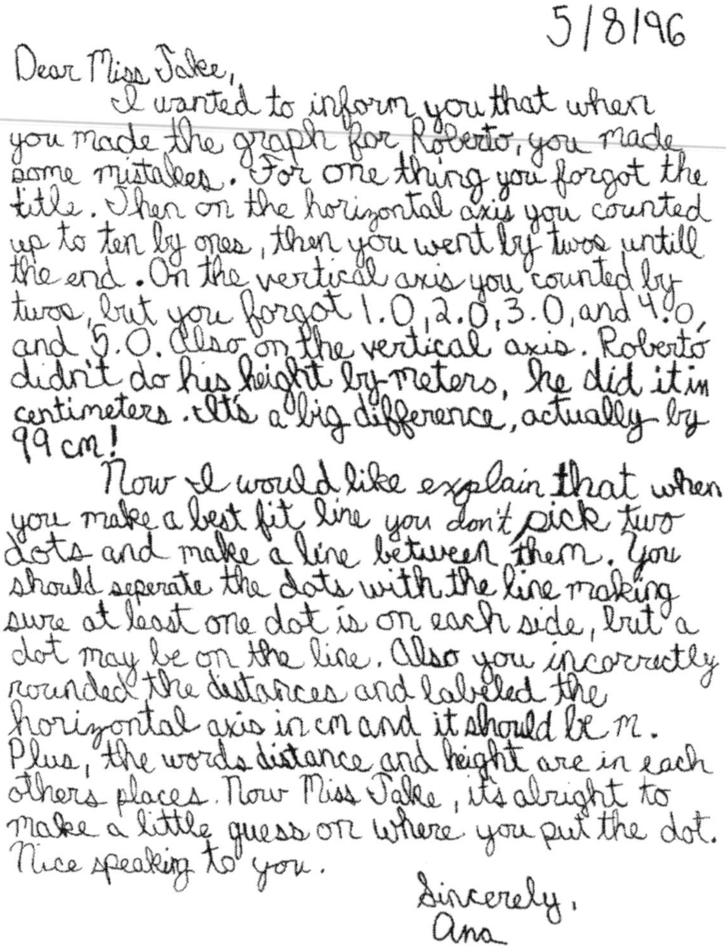

5/8/96

Dear Miss Take,
    I wanted to inform you that when you made the graph for Roberto, you made some mistakes. For one thing you forgot the title. Then on the horizontal axis you counted up to ten by ones, then you went by twos untill the end. On the vertical axis you counted by twos, but you forgot 1.0, 2.0, 3.0, and 4.0, and 5.0. Also on the vertical axis. Roberto didn't do his height by meters, he did it in centimeters. It's a big difference, actually by 99 cm!
    Now I would like explain that when you make a best fit line you don't pick two dots and make a line between them. You should seperate the dots with the line making sure at least one dot is on each side, but a dot may be on the line. Also you incorrectly rounded the distances and labeled the horizontal axis in cm and it should be m. Plus, the words distance and height are in each others places. Now Miss Take, its alright to make a little guess on where you put the dot. Nice speaking to you.
               Sincerely,
               Ana

Figure 12: *Sample student work for the Homework in the* Student Guide

AT A GLANCE

Math Facts and Daily Practice and Problems

DPP Bit Q practices division facts. Items O, P, R, S, and U all provide practice with decimals and build number sense. Items T and V build decimal understanding through metric measurement.

Before the Lab

Students bring in toy cars and roller skates. They select good rollers to use in the experiment.

Part 1. Beginning the Investigation

1. Set up two ramps with different heights to begin the discussion of the lab.
2. Introduce Jackie and Derrick's experiment by reading together the first page of the *Downhill Racer* Lab Pages in the *Student Guide*.
3. Discuss *Questions 1–3* in the *Student Guide* which will guide students in planning their experiment. Include fixed variables in your discussion. *(Question 2)*
4. Students identify the manipulated and responding variables in the experiment. *(Questions 4* and *5)*
5. Students draw pictures of the lab setup. Key variables should be indicated.

Part 2. Gathering and Organizing the Data

1. Set up as many ramps as space and materials allow.
2. Students work in groups of three to four to collect their data. *(Question 6)*
3. They record their data on a copy of a *Three-trial Data Table. (Question 7A)*
4. Discuss why taking an average of the data for the three trials is a good idea. *(Question 7B)*

Part 3. Graphing the Data and Analyzing the Results

1. Students graph their data on a copy of *Centimeter Graph Paper. (Question 8)*
2. Students use their data to answer *Questions 9–11.* These questions require predictions to be checked which may require the use of ramps again.

Part 4. Explore Questions

Students complete *Questions 14–19* individually or in small groups.

Homework

1. Assign some or all of the questions in the Explore section for homework.
2. Assign the Homework section on the *Downhill Racer* Lab Pages after students have completed the *Roberto's Data* Assessment Blackline Master.

Assessment

1. Use *Roberto's Data* Assessment Blackline Master to assess students' understanding of the Downhill Racer lab.
2. Use the *Observational Assessment Record* to document students' abilities to collect, organize, graph, and analyze data.
3. Transfer information from the Unit 10 *Observational Assessment Record* to students' *Individual Assessment Record Sheets*.

Notes:

Roberto's Data

You will need a sheet of *Centimeter Graph Paper* and a ruler.

Roberto did *Downhill Racer.* This is his data:

H Ramp Height (in cm)	D Distance Rolled (in m)			
	Trial 1	Trial 2	Trial 3	Average
8	0.97	0.93	0.95	
16	1.75	1.79	1.80	
24	3.01	2.97	2.90	

1. Find the median distance (*D*) for each height. Write your answers in the table.

2. Why did Roberto carry out three trials for each height?

3. Graph Roberto's data. Remember a title, labels, and units.

4. Fit a line to Roberto's data.

Use your graph of Roberto's data to answer these questions:

5. If the ramp height were 4 cm, how far would Roberto's car roll?

6. If the ramp height were 20 cm, how far would Roberto's car roll?

7. If Roberto's car rolled 2.5 m, what was the height of the ramp?

8. Roberto wants his car to roll 3.5 meters. What should Roberto do so that his car rolls 3.5 meters?

9. Roberto's friend Keenya used Roberto's car and ramp to collect her data. Keenya moved her starting line higher than Roberto's. Do you think Keenya's car rolled farther than Roberto's? Why or why not?

10. What do you think Keenya's graph would look like? Would her line be above or below Roberto's? Draw a line on your graph and label it "Keenya's Data."

Student Guide

Questions 1–19 (SG pp. 289–294)

1. Answers will vary.

2. *See the list of fixed variables in Lesson Guide 4. Car, ramp surface, floor surface, starting line, measuring points, etc.

3. Three or more trials for each height is a good idea since experimental and measurement errors as well as mistakes are inevitable. Gross errors can be checked. If the distance for one trial is very different from the other trials, that data should be thrown out and the trial should be repeated.

4. *the height (H) of the ramp

5. *the distance (D) the car rolls

6. Answers will vary, but paragraphs should include all the variables students hold fixed in order to make the experiment fair. For example, each group should describe the car they use, the starting line on their ramp, etc.

7. **A.** *See Figure 10 in Lesson Guide 4.

   B. *It is a good idea to find the average distance to average out any experimental and measurement error.

8. See Figure 11 in Lesson Guide 4.

Answers to *Questions 9–12* are based on the sample data and graph in Lesson Guide 4. Students' answers will vary based on their data.

9. **A.** Predicted D = 3.15 m

   B. interpolate

   C. Answers will vary.

   D. *Answers will vary.

10. **A.** 5 m

    B. extrapolate

    C. Answers will vary.

    D. *Answers will vary.

11. **A.** 5 cm. Find 1.5 cm on the vertical axis of the graph; draw a line horizontally until it reaches the best-fit line; draw a vertical line down until it reaches the horizontal axis. The point (5 cm) at which the vertical line touches the horizontal axis is the predicted height of the ramp.

    B. *Answers will vary.

12. *Line A. If the starting point were lower on the ramp, the car would not travel as far and the line would not be as steep as the line for the experiment.

13. **A.** Yes

    B. Yes

    C. The distance increases.

14. **A.** Starting Distance (S)

    B. Distance the car rolls (D)

    C. Possible answers: height of the ramp, car

    D. numerical

15. **A.** 85 cm

    B. 84 cm

16. **A.** 185 cm

    B. 187 cm

17.

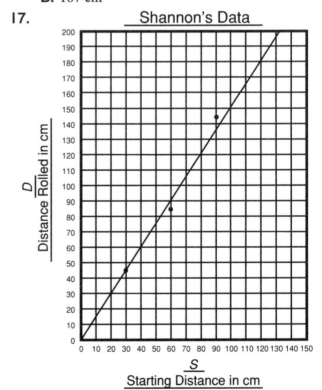

Shannon's Data

Distance D Rolled in cm (vertical axis)

Starting Distance S in cm (horizontal axis)

---

*Answers and/or discussion are included in the Lesson Guide.

**Answers for all the Home Practice in the *Discovery Assignment Book* are at the end of the unit.

18. A. About 70 cm. (Answers may vary slightly due to differences in best-fit lines and scales.)

B. interpolation

19. A. About 180 cm. (Answers may vary somewhat due to differences in best-fit lines and scales.)

B. extrapolation

Homework (SG p. 295)

Student paragraphs should include descriptions of the following mistakes:

• The horizontal axis should be labeled with Height (*H*), not Distance (*D*).

• The vertical axis should be labeled with Distance (*D*).

• There is no title.

• The points from Roberto's data are plotted incorrectly.

• The best-fit line is incorrect. It should take into account the point for *H* = 24 cm. The line should go above the two lower points and below the third point.

• The horizontal axis is scaled by ones to 10, then is scaled by twos.

• The vertical axis scale is missing 1.0, 2.0, 3.0, 4.0, and 4.4.

Unit Resource Guide

Roberto's Data (URG pp. 74–75)

Questions 1–10

1. Data table averages:
0.95
1.79
2.97

2. Answers will vary. Roberto carried out 3 trials to check for mistakes in data collection and to average out small errors.

3.–4.

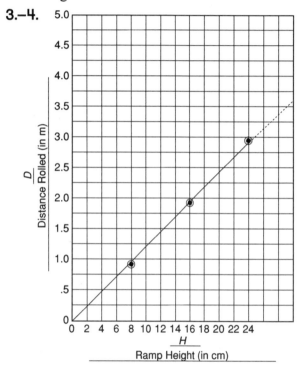

5. 0.5 m (Answers may vary somewhat due to differences in best-fit lines and scales.)

6. 2.4 m (Answers may vary slightly due to differences in best-fit lines and scales.)

7. 21 cm

8. Roberto should raise the ramp to about 29 cm.

9. A higher starting line would allow the car to roll longer and start at a greater height, so the car will roll farther.

10. Keenya's line will be above Roberto's.

---

*Answers and/or discussion are included in the Lesson Guide.

**Answers for all the Home Practice in the *Discovery Assignment Book* are at the end of the unit.

OPTIONAL LESSON

There are no Daily Practice and
Problems items for this lesson.

Decimal Hex

Estimated Class Sessions: 1

Students move two tokens to travel across
a game board by correctly comparing two
decimal fractions or a decimal and a common fraction.

Key Content

*   Comparing and ordering decimal fractions.
*   Translating between a common and a decimal
    fraction.

Curriculum Sequence

Before This Unit

In Grade 3 Unit 15, students were introduced to
this game.

Materials List

Print Materials for Students

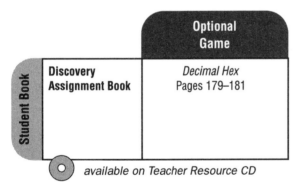

Student Book

Discovery Assignment Book

Optional Game

Decimal Hex
Pages 179–181

○ *available on Teacher Resource CD*

*All Transparency Masters, Blackline Masters,
and Assessment Blackline Masters in the
Unit Resource Guide are on the
Teacher Resource CD.*

Supplies for Each Student

clear plastic spinner or paper clip and pencil
base-ten pieces
2 same color centimeter cubes as game markers

Materials for the Teacher

Observational Assessment Record (Unit Resource Guide, Pages 9–10 and Teacher Resource CD)

Developing the Activity

To begin, students read directions on the *Decimal Hex* Game Pages in the *Discovery Assignment Book*. Each player places two same color centimeter cubes on two matching hexagons with the same number. The goal is to get the two cubes to the matching hexagons with the same number on the opposite side of the board. To move, a player spins the spinner. If the spinner shows greater than or equal to, the player can move to an adjacent hexagon with a number that is greater than or equal to his or her current position. If the spinner shows less than or equal to, the player moves to an adjacent hexagon with a number that is less than or equal to his or her current position. Students can model the decimals and fractions with base-ten pieces and use the pieces to make comparisons.

Suggestions for Teaching the Lesson

Homework and Practice

Encourage students to take home *Decimal Hex* to play with their families. Students will need their *Decimal Hex* Game Pages from the *Discovery Assignment Book*.

Assessment

Use the *Observational Assessment Record* to note students' abilities to compare and order decimals.

Name _____ Date _____

Decimal Hex

This is a game for two or three players.

Materials
- *Decimal Hex* Game Board on the following page
- two same color centimeter cubes or other game markers for each player
- one clear plastic spinner or pencil and paper clip

Rules
The goal of this game is to move two cubes or other markers from matching hexagons to opposite matching hexagons that all have the same number.

1. Each player places both of his or her cubes on two matching hexagons with the same number. The target hexagons are the matching ones with the same number on the other side of the game board.

2. The first player spins the spinner.

3. If "Greater Than or Equal To" shows, the player can move one cube to a neighboring hexagon with a number that is greater than or equal to the number in the hexagon where the cube is now.

4. If "Less Than or Equal To" shows, the player can move one cube to a neighboring hexagon with a number that is less than or equal to the number in the hexagon where the cube is now.

5. The player does not have to move a cube during his or her turn.

6. More than one cube can be on the same hexagon at the same time.

7. Players take turns spinning the spinner and moving cubes.

8. The first player to get both cubes to his or her target hexagons is the winner.

Decimal Hex   DAB · Grade 4 · Unit 10 · Lesson 5 179

Discovery Assignment Book - Page 179

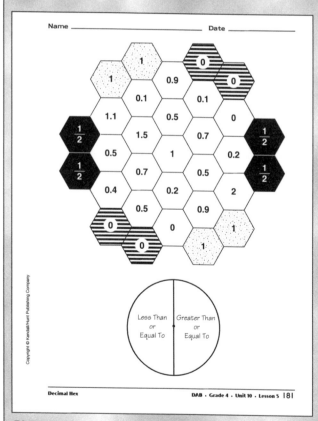

Name _____ Date _____

Decimal Hex   DAB · Grade 4 · Unit 10 · Lesson 5 181

Discovery Assignment Book - Page 181

AT A GLANCE

Developing the Activity

1. Students read the rules on the *Decimal Hex* Game Pages in the *Discovery Assignment Book*.
2. Students play *Decimal Hex*.

Homework

Students take home the *Decimal Hex* Game Pages. They play the game with family members.

Assessment

Use the *Observational Assessment Record* to note students' abilities to compare and order decimals.

Notes:

LESSON GUIDE 6

Alberto in TenthsLand

Estimated Class Sessions: 1

Alberto falls asleep in the library and has a dream about a place called TenthsLand. He has a series of adventures in which he meets the Ten Percent Taxer, the Tenth-i-Pede, and the Centimeter Ruler. His dream ends when Mrs. Carroll, the librarian, gently shakes him awake.

Key Content

- Finding 10 percent of a number.
- Measuring to the nearest tenth of a centimeter.
- Multiplying by ten and by one-tenth.

Key Vocabulary

10%

Daily Practice and Problems: Bit for Lesson 6

W. Quiz on 2s and 3s Division Facts
(URG p. 25)

A. $8 \div 2 =$	B. $30 \div 3 =$
C. $16 \div 2 =$	D. $9 \div 3 =$
E. $12 \div 2 =$	F. $21 \div 3 =$
G. $15 \div 3 =$	H. $4 \div 2 =$
I. $10 \div 2 =$	J. $27 \div 3 =$
K. $14 \div 2 =$	L. $12 \div 3 =$
M. $6 \div 3 =$	N. $24 \div 3 =$
O. $2 \div 1 =$	P. $18 \div 3 =$
Q. $18 \div 2 =$	R. $3 \div 3 =$
S. $20 \div 2 =$	

DPP Task is on page 87. Suggestions for using the DPPs are on page 87.

Materials List

Print Materials for Students

		Math Facts and Daily Practice and Problems	Activity	Homework	Written Assessment
Student Books	**Adventure Book**		*TenthsLand* Pages 45–56		
	Discovery Assignment Book			Home Practice Part 6 Page 158	
Teacher Resources	**Facts Resource Guide** ⊙	DPP Items 10W & 10X			DPP Item 10W *Quiz on 2s and 3s Division Facts*
	Unit Resource Guide	DPP Items W–X Page 25 ⊙			DPP Item W *Quiz on 2s and 3s Division Facts* Page 25 ⊙

⊙ *available on Teacher Resource CD*

All Transparency Masters, Blackline Masters, and Assessment Blackline Masters in the Unit Resource Guide are on the Teacher Resource CD.

Supplies for Each Student

calculator

This story is based on *Alice in Wonderland,* especially her adventures when she follows the White Rabbit down the rabbit hole. Students familiar with Alice may enjoy this story more.

IMS Tip

You may want to read the story twice—once for the basic plot, and once again to draw out the mathematics.

Alberto in TenthsLand

Alberto was reading a book in the library when it happened. The book was about basketball, Alberto's favorite game, but Alberto had played basketball all morning, and he was feeling sleepy and dull. He had begun to wonder how high a basketball would bounce if it were dropped from the rim, 10 feet up. He didn't know how he could find out since he couldn't reach that high to drop the ball. He thought the problem was like something he had done in school, but he couldn't remember exactly what.

Then he saw it. A small white mouse ran across the library floor and disappeared into a heating vent. Seeing a mouse was not unusual since the library was old. Alberto was not even especially surprised to see that this mouse was dressed in sweats and high-tops. But when the mouse pulled out a calculator and started pushing buttons furiously as he scurried along, Alberto jumped up and hurried after him.

46   AB · Grade 4 · Unit 10 · Lesson 6

Adventure Book - Page 46

Page 46

- *What experiment might Alberto be thinking of?*

Bouncing Ball

- *How could he predict how high a basketball would bounce if it were dropped from 10 feet?*

Gather data for lesser heights, graph it, and extrapolate. Or, drop it from 5 feet and double the bounce height.

- *What could the white mouse be doing with a calculator?*

Discussion Prompts

Page 47

- *What do you notice about the trees in TenthsLand? What about the sun?*

The trees are divided into ten parts. The sun has ten points.

- *Why does that make sense in a place called TenthsLand?*

Because tenths require dividing things into ten parts.

Alberto in TenthsLand

After the mouse disappeared into the heating vent, Alberto paused hardly a moment before crawling in himself. He crawled down a tunnel for a few meters. Then, suddenly, he found himself falling down, down, down.

He fell for what seemed a very long time, but at last he landed gently on a pile of crumpled newspapers. He was just able to see the white mouse hurry off down a narrow path through the woods.

AB · Grade 4 · Unit 10 · Lesson 6   47

Adventure Book - Page 47

Page 48

- *What do you think the Ten-X-Sizer might do?*
- *Why is Alberto saying good-bye to his feet?*

Because they are getting to be so far away.

Alberto in TenthsLand

Alberto jumped up and started down the path after the white mouse. He hadn't gone far when he came to a clearing in the woods. He was just in time to see the white mouse disappear through a very small door in a tree.

Alberto hurried over to the door and kneeled down to take a peek. Through the door he saw a wonderful garden. Alberto was bitterly disappointed that he was far too big to fit through the door.

When Alberto stood up, he was surprised to see a strange machine in the clearing—he was sure it hadn't been there before. The machine looked like a small rocket launch pad with a tower. On the side of the tower was written "Ten-X-Sizer" and on the top was a button labeled "Push me."

Alberto stood on the pad and looked at the button. Now, Alberto was always careful with machines, and he knew that pushing buttons could sometimes cause trouble, so he looked all around to see if there were any signs labeled "Danger." He found none, so he decided to push the button. The next thing Alberto knew his head was poking up past the tops of the trees all around and his feet were rapidly disappearing. "Good-bye, feet. Be good," thought Alberto as he grew and grew and grew.

48   AB · Grade 4 · Unit 10 · Lesson 6

Adventure Book - Page 48

The view from high above the trees was lovely, but now Alberto was farther than ever from being able to get through the tiny door and into the wonderful garden. The disappointment was too much for poor Alberto, and he began to cry. He sat down and shed huge tears.

After a few minutes of crying, Alberto noticed another machine in the clearing—and he wondered why he hadn't noticed this one before either. This machine was very much like the first machine; only the words on the tower were different. On the new machine was written, "Tenth-X-Sizer."

AB · Grade 4 · Unit 10 · Lesson 6   49

Adventure Book - Page 49

Alberto thought that he might as well try this machine too, as he figured he could be no worse off than he was already. It was hard for him to fit on the machine, but as soon as he pushed the button he felt himself shrinking, shrinking, shrinking. In a moment, he was back to his proper size.

"If one push can do so much," thought Alberto, "I wonder what another will do." Alberto pushed the Tenth-X-Sizer button again and to his delight found himself shrinking once more. Luckily, he did not shrink away to nothing, but stopped at just the perfect height to fit through the tiny door in the tree. Immediately, Alberto went through the door and found himself in the beautiful garden.

50   AB · Grade 4 · Unit 10 · Lesson 6

Adventure Book - Page 50

Discussion Prompts

Page 49

- *How tall would you be if you were ten times as tall? As tall as the ceiling? As tall as the school building? A tree? A skyscraper?*

Fourth graders are normally between 50 and 60 inches. Since $10 \times 55 = 550$ inches or about 46 feet, this could be the height of a building.

- *How long would your foot be? Draw a picture of your ten-times-as-long footprint.*
- *How long would your pencil be?*
- *What do you think the Tenth-X-Sizer will do?*

Page 50

- *How tall would you be if you were one-tenth as tall as you are now? Find an object in the classroom that is close to this height.*

Fourth graders are about 55 inches tall. One-tenth of 55 inches is 5.5 inches, so look for objects that are between 5 and 6 inches such as a calculator or a sharpened pencil.

- *How long would your foot be? How long would your pencil be?*
- *How many times could Alberto push the Tenth-X-Sizer button before he shrank to nothing?*

No matter how many times he pushed the button, he would never become nothing. He would get smaller and smaller, but there would always be a little bit left.

Discussion Prompts

Page 51

- *Why does the Ten Percent Taxer have 1040 written on him?*

That's the number of the form for filing federal income tax returns in the United States.

- *What do you notice about the Ten Percent Taxer?*

He's divided into ten parts.

- *What do people really get for the taxes they pay?*

Schools, roads, national defense, help for poor people, foreign aid, food inspection, environmental protection, parks, police, etc.

- *What is 10 percent of the things Alberto has?*

Discuss with students that 10% means 10 out of 100 or one-tenth. Students can find 10% of the items by using a calculator to divide by 10. Students who completed Unit 6 Lesson 5 can also move the decimal point one place to the left and round or truncate the answer.

He has 22 marbles, 39¢, 11 pieces of gum, and some string. Ten percent of these is roughly two marbles, 4¢, and one piece of gum. To find 10 percent of the string, the Ten Percent Taxer will have to fold it into ten equal parts or measure it.

- *What is 10 percent of 30 marbles? Of 70¢? Of 150 cm?*

3 marbles, 7¢, 15 cm. Repeat for other amounts.

Page 53

- *What animal does the Tenth-i-Pede's name remind you of?*

Centipede.

- *What do the word parts of centipede mean?*

Centi- is from the Latin for 100; *pede* is from the Latin word for foot. A centipede doesn't really have 100 feet, but it does have quite a few.

- *What other words can you think of that have cent- in them?*

Centimeter, cent, centigrade, century.

- *What do those words mean?*

$\frac{1}{100}$ of a meter, $\frac{1}{100}$ of a dollar, a temperature scale with 100 degrees between the freezing and boiling temperatures of water, a period of 100 years.

"Stop!" cried an odd creature who looked like a large piece of paper. "I am the Ten Percent Taxer. Pay your taxes at once or go to jail!"

"Taxes?" replied Alberto. "What are taxes?"

"Taxes buy civilization," answered the Ten Percent Taxer. "Now, show me what you have and I will take 10 percent. You must pay $\frac{1}{10}$ of what you have."

Alberto emptied his pockets. He had a bag of marbles, a quarter, a dime, four pennies, a half-empty package of chewing gum, and some kite string.

AB · Grade 4 · Unit 10 · Lesson 6 51

Adventure Book - Page 51

Alberto gathered up his other things and looked around. He was startled to see what looked like a large caterpillar on the branch of a nearby tree. It seemed that the creature had been watching for some time.

"Who are you?" asked the creature.

"I'm not quite sure," answered Alberto. "I know who I was this morning when I got up, but I've changed several times since then, and now I'm not sure anymore. Who are you?"

"I'm the Tenth-i-Pede," replied the creature, who was beginning to disappear. The last three tenths were already gone and several more were fading fast. "If you don't know who you are, do you at least know what you're doing?"

Alberto answered, "I'm trying to find the white mouse. Have you seen him?"

"White mouse?" repeated the Tenth-i-Pede, who by this time was almost entirely gone. "White mouse? Look for the Centimeter Ruler. The white mouse works for her." And with that, the Tenth-i-Pede faded away the rest of the way, except for a faint outline of his smile, which lingered a minute or two longer.

AB · Grade 4 · Unit 10 · Lesson 6 53

Adventure Book - Page 53

"Come here, stand next to me!" shouted the Centimeter Ruler.
"Now, Mr. Mouse, how tall is he?"

"About 24 cm," answered the white mouse.

"You ninny! He's nowhere near 24 cm!" shouted the Centimeter Ruler.

"I meant to say that 10 percent of the string is about 24 cm," answered the mouse. "This fellow looks about 15.6 cm tall."

"Now, that's more like it!" shouted the Centimeter Ruler. "Now, you, Ten Percent Taxer, get his shirt and pants—we need 10 percent of those too."

At that, the Ten Percent Taxer and the Centimeter Ruler began to grab Alberto's shirt, trying to pull it off.

"No! No!" shouted Alberto.
"That's my shirt. Leave me alone!"

The Centimeter Ruler, the Ten Percent Taxer, and the white mouse all tugged and pulled at Alberto's shirt. Alberto gave a shout of anger and tried to beat them off. Then he found himself sitting back in the library. Mrs. Carroll, the librarian, was gently shaking his shoulder. "Wake up! Alberto, wake up!" she said. "You've been asleep for a very long time. You must go now; we're closing."

AB · Grade 4 · Unit 10 · Lesson 6   55

Adventure Book - Page 55

"Oh! What an amazing dream!" said Alberto as he gathered his books and hurried home to tell his mother about his strange dream.

Mrs. Carroll shook her head and smiled. Then, as she was closing up for the night, she saw a small white mouse scurry into an old heat vent. "How odd," she thought, "for a moment it looked as though that mouse was wearing sweats and high-tops."

56   AB · Grade 4 · Unit 10 · Lesson 6

Adventure Book - Page 56

Discussion Prompts

Page 55

- *What is 10 percent of 237 cm?*

About 24 cm. Exactly, 23.7 cm.

- *What is 10 percent of 250 cm? Of 500 cm?*

25 cm, 50 cm. Repeat for other lengths.

Page 56

- *Why is the librarian named Mrs. Carroll?*

Because the pseudonym of Charles Dodgson, author of *Alice in Wonderland,* was Lewis Carroll, and this story is based on some of Alice's adventures.

Suggestions for Teaching the Lesson

Math Facts

DPP Task X asks students to solve a division problem, write a story about it, and draw a picture.

Homework and Practice

* Read and discuss the Adventure Book with someone at home.

* Assign Part 6 of the Home Practice.

Answers for Part 6 of the Home Practice can be found in the Answer Key at the end of this lesson and at the end of this unit.

Assessment

DPP Bit W is a short quiz on the division facts for the twos and threes.

Literature Connection

* Carroll, Lewis. *The Annotated Alice: The Definitive Edition. Alice's Adventures in Wonderland;* and *Through the Looking-Glass and What Alice Found There.* Introduction by Martin Gardner. Illustrated by John Tenniel. W.W. Norton & Company, New York, 1999.

Daily Practice and Problems: Task for Lesson 6

X. Task: Dividing It Up (URG p. 25)

$26 \div 8 = ?$ Write a story for $26 \div 8$. Then, draw a picture. Include any remainder in your picture.

Name _____ Date _____

Part 6 **Playing at the Park**

1. **A.** When Shannon and her family arrived at the park on Saturday, Shannon counted 3 children on *each* of the following: the slide, the swings, the monkey bars, and the merry-go-round. How many children were at the park when Shannon arrived?

   B. If there were 8 more children than adults at the park, how many adults were at the park?

2. A used car dealer is across the street from the park. Shannon's dad looked at some cars while Shannon and her sister played at the park. He liked two different cars. One car costs $4550 and the other costs $3775. What is the difference in price of the two cars?

3. Shannon treated her little sister and her mother to a treat. At a nearby stand she bought two cans of juice at 65¢ each and three popsicles at 85¢ each. She gave the vendor $5.00. How much change will Shannon receive?

4. While playing in the park, Shannon's family saw a 5 kilometer race. 235 people were signed up to participate, but only 178 arrived the day of the race. How many people did not show up for the race?

5. **A.** Last summer, the park district raised money for new playground equipment. In June, $565 was raised. In July, $438 was raised. In August, $395 was raised. How much money was raised for new playground equipment?

   B. How much money do they need to raise in September to reach their goal of $1500?

158 DAB · Grade 4 · Unit 10   USING DECIMALS

Discovery Assignment Book - Page 158

Discovery Assignment Book

**Home Practice (DAB p. 158)

Part 6. Playing at the Park

Questions 1–5

1. **A.** 12 children

    B. 4 adults

2. $775

3. $1.15

4. 57 people

5. **A.** $1398

    B. $102

*Answers and/or discussion are included in the Lesson Guide.

**Answers for all the Home Practice in the *Discovery Assignment Book* are at the end of the unit.

88   **URG · Grade 4 · Unit 10 · Lesson 6 · Answer Key**

Discovery Assignment Book

Part 2. Missing Numbers and Big Numbers

Questions 1–3 (DAB p. 155)

1. **A.** $n = 4$
   B. $n = 6$
   C. $n = 30$
   D. $n = 200$
   E. $n = 30$
   F. $n = 3$

2. **A.** 45,089; 45,676; 45,788; 47,998; 48,654; 54,673
   B. 49,000
   C. 45,100

3. Answers will vary. Possible answers are:
   A. $600,000 + 30,000 = 630,000$
   B. $2,700,000 + 4,000,000 = 6,700,000$
   C. $400,000 - 100,000 = 300,000$

Part 3. Decimals

Questions 1–3 (DAB p. 156)

1. **A.** 3.3
   B. 3.6
   C. 3.03
   D. 4.4
   3.03; 3.3; 3.6; 4.4

2. Answers will vary.

3. **A.** 1 dm, 23 cm, 0.45 m, 0.6 m, 55 dm
   B. 1.03 m, 1.24 m, 1.5 m, 1 m and 8 dm

Part 4. School Supplies

Questions 1–4 (DAB p. 157)

1. $3 \times \$0.40 = \$1.20$;
   $\$1.20 + \$3 + \$0.10 + \$2 = \$6.30$

2. $5 \times \$0.40 = \$2$;
   $\$2 + \$3 + \$0.30 + \$1 = \$6.30$

3. Linda: $6.25
   Linda's brother: $6.23

4. $\$6.25 - \$6.23 = \$0.02$ or 2¢

Part 5. Addition, Subtraction, and Multiplication

Questions 1–3 (DAB p. 157)

1. **A.** 19   **B.** 234
   C. 522   **D.** 235
   E. 423   **F.** 182
   G. 306   **H.** 184

2. Possible strategy: 26×7 is close to 25×7. Skip count by 25s seven times: 25, 50, 75, 100, 125, 150, 175. 26×7 is about 175.

3. Possible strategy: $432 - 197$ is the same as $435 - 200 = 235$.

Part 6. Playing at the Park

Questions 1–5 (DAB p. 158)

1. **A.** 12 children
   B. 4 adults

2. $775

3. $1.15

4. 57 people

5. **A.** $1398
   B. $102

---

*Answers and/or discussion are included in the Lesson Guide.